Jonathan was a wonderful innovator who was constantly bringing new people into the business and coming up with new ideas, most notably the Cartier Million. However, his most enduring legacy must surely be the work he has done and continues to do for the Jack and Jill Foundation.

John Magnier, Coolmore Stud

Jack & Jill

The Story of Jonathan Irwin

JONATHAN IRWIN

with Emily Hourican

MERCIER PRESS
IRISH PUBLISHER – IRISH STORY

MERCIER PRESS

Cork

www.mercierpress.ie

© Text: Jonathan Irwin, 2014

© Introduction: Denis O'Brien, 2014

ISBN: 978 1 78117 233 9

10 9 8 7 6 5 4 3 2 1

A CIP record for this title is available from the British Library

Printed and bound in the EU.

For John, Jack and Samson Fortune

This book is inspired by all the wonderful people whose paths have crossed mine throughout my life. Some are mentioned here by name, many others are not, but their influence and importance have been no less for that. If some dates and facts are slightly loose, the fault is entirely that of my memory.

My special thanks to Emily Hourican for her help and hard work in preparing this story for publication.

All profits from this book will go to the Jack & Jill Children's Foundation.

CONTENTS

A NOTE FROM THE EDITOR

As a journalist and editor, combining work with bringing up three children, I first came across Jack and Jill in 2009, when I heard Jonathan tell the story of Jack's life and death at a conference. I was deeply moved by what he said and by his dedication to helping other children like Jack. So when he suggested I might like to help write this book, I jumped at the chance to tell such a great story.

Emily Hourican
April 2014

INTRODUCTION

BY DENIS O'BRIEN

I first met Jonathan Irwin when I was about fourteen. My father had known him for years and held him in very high regard. Jonathan had just been appointed CEO of Goffs Bloodstock, who were in the process of opening their spanking new sales facility in County Kildare. At the same time, my father had just set up his equine supplementation business. Jonathan, recognising that my father needed a leg up with his fledgling business, very graciously allowed him to pepper the sales ring with signs for Plusvital, as well as showing off his product range in pride of place on the balcony above the sales ring, all for no charge. When I saw how much help my father had been given, I remember thinking that this man was different and had a great human touch about him.

A few years later, I witnessed Jonathan's great flair for marketing when he brought the Cartier Million to the Phoenix Park Racecourse, setting him apart as one of the great marketers in Ireland during the 1980s and 1990s. Much later, I had the privilege of working with him during my time as chair of the 2003 Special Olympics World Games organising committee, with Jonathan as venues director. Jonathan was head of the Dublin Sports Council and we worked closely in preparation for the World Games.

In the intervening time, Jonathan had turned his attention to children with severe disabilities and had set up the Jack and Jill Foundation on whose board I served for a number of years. Jonathan is a very practical man, but when it comes to creativity and new ways to fund the organisation he is quite brilliant. Some of his initiatives for raising money for Jack and Jill have been outstanding.

However, it is Jonathan's response to adversity that sets him apart. I remember the terrible impact on him when his newborn son Jack was left with severe brain damage, and much later when another son, Sam, tragically died in an accident in Portugal. What struck me most about Jonathan was his dignity in dealing with both of those tragedies. Instead of asking 'Why me?' and lamenting the hand that fate had dealt him, Jonathan got on with the role of supporting others – Mary-Ann, Mikaela and his other children – and of trying to find some kind of positive outcome from the tragedies.

With the Jack and Jill Foundation, he succeeded in establishing a charity that has made a huge difference to many lives, challenged government policy and been an advocate for children with brain damage who had no one else to speak for them – all of which is a remarkable achievement.

A successful charity is probably the hardest business to set up, as most do not manage to make it out of the starting blocks. However, the Jack and Jill Foundation has gone from being the dream of grieving parents – that no other family should suffer the way he and Mary-Ann did when they discovered there were no support services to help them cope with their son – to become the first port of call for families in similar trouble, and a substantial buffer between those families and the desperate exhaustion that Jonathan and Mary-Ann faced.

All of the things that made Jonathan so successful in the early part of his life – his skill and vision at marketing, his infectious enthusiasm, considerable charm and integrity – have been brought to bear on his work with the Foundation. Without his experience and talent, Jack and Jill would never have taken off. I am fairly sure that its continuing success means more to him than all the other accolades of his career.

Jonathan is great company and makes friends wherever he goes – it is no surprise that he is the only person to be twice elected Personality of the Year by the Irish Breeders' Association. He is unfailingly polite and courteous. His manners are based on a genuine regard for other people – their comfort and their happiness. His roots are in Ireland and his contributions to this country have been very genuine. Despite his plummy Eton tones, Jonathan has always had a great love of Ireland and a great belief in the country. He is as Irish as they come. His vision for the Irish bloodstock industry has largely been realised. His determination that Ireland could attract significant sporting events was steadfast at a time when there was little in terms of infrastructure to substantiate this belief. He is inclined to be modest and humorous about his achievements, but let none of us be beguiled by his demeanour. His achievements are remarkable. Tragedy, when it came, did not defeat him – it transformed him, which should be an inspiration for the rest of us.

1

FATHER AND GRANDFATHER

Although I grew up in England and led a very English life –
school in Kent and then at Eton, followed by a year working
in television in London – from the earliest age I had a strong
feeling for Ireland, of being involved here and belonging here,
presumably because of my Irish background.

My paternal grandfather, Dr Thomas Irwin, was a great
educationalist. From 1900 he was a teacher at Wesley College,
a Methodist boarding and day school in the centre of Dublin,
and principal from 1910 to 1945. One of the first things he
did as principal was to admit girls, on the very sound basis
that 'there is no doubt co-education cultivates greater mutual
knowledge and respect and those best qualified to judge assert
that the moral tone is higher than where boys and girls are
educated separately'. He bought the site that now houses the
Burlington Hotel, and his original plan was to start a girls'
school there. However, instead, that site was sold, and it made
Wesley College a fortune, allowing it to build the rather ugly
campus in Ballinteer and move there from its original home on
St Stephen's Green.

Grandfather was not particularly tall, but I remember him

as being very elegant. He always carried a silver cane, wore a top hat, spats, gaiters and a frock coat, and was easily recognised around Dublin. He was also an enormously good preacher – I went to one or two of the services he gave when I was a boy. I imagine with a name like Irwin, the family must originally have come from Northern Ireland, and my grandmother, his second wife – she was the only wife I knew, his first wife having died before I was born – was also from Northern Ireland. She was quite a cold woman. Her maiden name was Nicholson and she was a niece of Brigadier-General Nicholson, a soldier of some genius who retook Delhi from the Indian mutineers, and a man so extreme and colourful that he appears in Rudyard Kipling's *Kim*, in George MacDonald Fraser's *Flashman* and in James Leasor's *Follow the Drum*. One famous story told about him is of a night during the mutiny when he strode into the British mess tent, coughed to attract the attention of the officers, then said, 'I am sorry, gentlemen, to have kept you waiting for your dinner, but I have been hanging your cooks.' He had been told that the regimental chefs had poisoned the soup with aconite. When they refused to taste it for him, he force-fed it to a monkey. When the monkey instantly died, Nicholson proceeded to hang the cooks from a nearby tree.

As a child, I usually came to Dublin once a year to see my grandparents. On my first visit, in 1941, I was only about three or four months old, and my mother Pippa brought me (at the height of the U-boat war, which was dangerous and daring of her) because I was such a thin, sickly infant and not thriving at all. She feared I wouldn't live and so brought me to see a brilliant doctor she had heard about, Dr Coleman Saunders. He took one look at me and said, 'The child is being starved to death; give him cow's milk by the ton.' Presumably he saved my life. It seemed my mother had no milk for me; once I was being given cow's milk, I became a healthy, chubby lad.

Grandfather died at ninety-five, and my recollections of him are of a very kindly man, someone I always looked forward to seeing. However, I don't think he had a particularly warm or loving relationship with his children. 'We didn't deserve our children, but they surely didn't deserve us,' was one of his sayings. Certainly, they were not close as a family. Grandfather had seven children including my father, John, and I still haven't met some of his brothers and sisters – my aunts and uncles. There was only one child by Thomas' first wife, a marvellous man, Colonel Jimmy Irwin, who served with great distinction in the Welsh Guards during the Great War. In the Second World War he was a colonel in the Gurkhas and fought the Japanese right through Burma. Later, he had a fruit farm at Stratford St Mary in Suffolk, which is where I met him, although not until I was fifteen. Before that, I didn't even know he existed. It was all a bit dysfunctional really and I don't think my father was especially close to any of his siblings except for his twin, Desmond. Desmond was a doctor, with a very successful psychiatric practice in Harley Street, whom I was very fond of. But we didn't see very much of him, even when we lived in London.

My father was very highly strung and he wasn't a great family man, whether it was with his brothers and sisters or his wife and child. And anyway, he wanted to escape. Dublin in the late 1930s was a very dull, depressing place – maybe all of Europe was at that stage? – but certainly for a man who had serious ambitions and a strong sense of himself, there wasn't much to hold him there. He wanted to get out, to make a name for himself, and he did. Asked by Grandfather after he finished school what he wanted to be, John apparently could only reply 'alive'.

He might have lacked direction, but John had nerve, determination and a measure of beginner's luck. He trained as an actor and was very much tied up with the Gate Theatre. He knew James Mason from that time; and Orson Welles, who had been travelling around Ireland in a horse-drawn caravan, painting, when he dropped in at the Gate and agreed to play the Duke in *Jew Süss*, apparently his first-ever performance in a professional theatre; Hilton Edwards and Micheál MacLiammóir, of course; Michael Scott; the playwright Denis Johnston; and Shelagh Richards – I think he lived with her on a barge on the Thames at Hammersmith in London for a short while. The barge had been built for Lillie Langtry and was elegant and comfortable, with a room for the housekeeper. But acting was never the height of John's ambition; it was more a means to an end. What really fascinated him was first radio and then television, and the potential of these. He understood them in a way that very few people did then, particularly television: the things that could be done with it, the creative opportunities it offered.

John's big break came when he played Johnny Boyle in the

first production of *Juno and the Paycock* to go to London, with Sarah Allgood as his mother and Arthur Sinclair as his father. The play travelled to the Royal Theatre, Haymarket, before the war and ran for many months. From there, John was put under contract to J. Arthur Rank, who created Pinewood Studios, then the biggest film production company in the UK. However, once war came the film industry virtually collapsed and my father started to work instead for BBC radio in Northern Ireland and London. The story he told of getting his first job, in Northern Ireland, is that Denis Johnston, who was a friend, took him out to dinner and suggested John join him as a radio producer in Belfast, because he was 'the right type', regardless of any actual experience. So John went to Belfast to meet the Appointments Board, where he found 'it was soon apparent that the board found me about as interesting as I found them', i.e., not at all. However, everything changed when the board asked John where they could get in touch with him.

'"At the moment I'm staying at — Castle," I said.'

'"But isn't that Lord —'s home?" asked one.'

That clinched it. John left the room knowing he had the job, with a salary of £300 a year.

At BBC Belfast, John created and produced *Ulster Weekly*, the first really popular show of the time, which generated more fan mail than any other programme produced anywhere by the BBC and was listened to in Scotland and Wales as well. He also met my mother in Belfast, while she was touring with the Molly Keane play *Spring Meeting*. This is John's account of it, as contained in *My Time is My Own*, a memoir of his time in radio and TV published in 1955: 'I went to see it and afterwards went round to meet my old friend Arthur Sinclair who introduced me to the leading lady, Miss Zena Dare … we continued through luncheon, where I met the very pretty ingénue of the company, Philippa Stanley-Clarke. Next week, when they had gone to continue their tour in Liverpool, I found this girl's face coming into my mind more frequently than was comfortable. I was too busy for such distraction and so sent a telegram, 'WILL YOU MARRY ME'. When I got her reply, 'YES PLEASE', I was able to concentrate on my work again. We were married on the following first of January, giving me no excuse to forget any of our anniversaries. Eighteen months later our son Jonathan was clever enough to be born on Midsummer's Day, thus making his birthday present equally secure.'

In fact, he was wrong. I was born a few days earlier, on 21 June, the longest day of the year, not Midsummer, which is 24 June. But at least he had the right month.

John also covered the Nuremberg trials for the *Irish Independent*, but he never really talked about that episode in his life, which is a shame, because I would have loved to have heard the inside story from someone so perfectly placed to observe Hitler's disciples. I think he was traumatised by the devastating detail of what he heard and didn't want to relive it.

After the war, John moved to London and became a television producer at the BBC, producing some of the biggest shows of the era: some brilliant, such as the Taylor history lectures, *The $64,000 Question* and *Kaleidoscope*, and some truly bad. He later also produced a series of shows for NBC in America, with Eleanor Roosevelt and then Bertrand Russell.

The bureaucracy of the BBC, the many unspoken rules around what could and couldn't be shown on TV, wore him down, and for a time he turned his back on it, directing six films for John Croydon, who had a small studio at Highbury. 'I know after directing six films how little I know about the cinema. I know how complex it is; I know how it terrifies me; and yet nothing has for me the fascination of this, the most difficult medium of them all,' he wrote in *My Time is My Own*. From there he returned to TV on a freelance basis, producing *In the News*, a seminal political show based on what John describes as 'the bare simplicity of two speakers of right-wing opinion facing two left-wing speakers across the neutral area of a plain table, with a chairman to keep them to the subject'. This was one of the great shows of its time, watched by everybody and often highly controversial. One night, after the show, John got a call from the Dowager Marchioness of Something, who berated him, 'You have done something that nobody has dared to do before. You have put a socialist in my drawing room. This is not to happen again. I am never at home to Mr Michael Foot or any of his misguided cronies.'

However, the show ran into trouble 'upstairs' because John always chose those politicians who were the best speakers and had the most charisma, rather than the soundest exponents of their party's views. The political parties began to complain, insisting that the show give time to the most reliable party politicians, rather than the best broadcasters. The BBC gave way to their protests and insisted that John choose on different criteria. As a result, the popularity of the show suffered and eventually it became fortnightly rather than weekly.

Somehow, John's career never seemed really to take off as it deserved. Despite dreaming up some wonderful ideas for shows, he found it difficult to work within the constraints of the BBC bureaucracy, finding them far too inclined to sacrifice free speech to expediency. The lack of competition, until the independent channels came along, didn't help either. Not only was there no incentive to be brave in the face of political interference, there wasn't even much of a push to get programmes out on time; I remember the ten o'clock news often went out, live, at about twenty minutes past ten.

During those years, my mother was asked one sports day at my prep school by another mother, 'What does your husband do?' to which she replied, after a judicious pause, 'Do you mean this week?' John wrote for newspapers and TV, directed films, produced TV programmes and sat on a few boards and committees. He chose his projects according to which was the most interesting rather than the best paid, and frequently turned down very lucrative offers because he didn't think there was anything to be learned from them, or thought there was insufficient chance of doing them as well as he would have liked. Or because they were unworthy, in his eyes. He insisted there was nothing quixotic about this attitude, but for a husband and father it was perhaps a little cavalier. My mother, still alive and well at ninety-five, says that actually John was mainly fascinated by himself; in his own eyes, he was the most compelling man around.

After the BBC, John was very instrumental in encouraging the creation of commercial television. He was excited by the creative possibilities of a freer kind of production and the opportunities it represented for younger people. He had a great gift with young people, to make them feel they weren't as inexperienced and hopeless as they probably felt they were, and to make them believe that they were actually talented. He gave them real chances, trusting that they would be able for the opportunities. When I came to Dublin first as a young man myself, I remember being struck by what a very old society this was, commercially. All power was in the hands of the elderly, and the feeling was that just because you were young, you weren't going to get the job. But my father had none of that. He encouraged young people, and achieved a great deal himself while he was still young.

I always noticed over the years, when we came back to Dublin from London, the slightly wary attitude my father's friends had towards him. He was ostentatious and mercurial. He could be in the money one year, because three of his shows were doing brilliantly, then the next year things would be very tough. He knew a lot of people, was always giving dinner parties in glamorous restaurants and going to the casinos, where he might make a fortune one day, then blow it all the next. I knew a lot of his old acting buddies in Dublin, and even at a young age I could see them being a bit edgy with him. Here was this pal of theirs, who'd done well for himself abroad, arriving in a Ford Zodiac convertible and wearing an astrakhan fur coat. He would have large lunch parties at the Red Bank, Jammet's restaurant or the Russell, and spent a lot of his time at the races. Meanwhile, they were probably still struggling, as most people who stayed in Ireland were, and I think they slightly resented it. Actually, I think there has always been a slight tension in this country between those who went abroad, particularly if they succeeded, and those who stayed behind.

John was a very fascinating person, but he was very fragile emotionally too. He was not at all domestic – I always got the impression that family and home weren't very interesting for him. The domestic stage was too small, too dull. He was amusing, an entertainer and an actor, always acting a part, even though he graduated to making TV shows rather than appearing in them. Socially, he had to be the tops, the shiniest and the most brilliant of all. My mother said that he had brains, but they were beside the point, not the main point. He was a very exciting father to have, but he was definitely a merchant venturer; being 'Daddy' just didn't fit with his plans. Any time I asked him, 'Couldn't we do such-and-such next weekend?' he would always say, 'We'll see,' but 'we'll see' never came to pass.

He tried to kill himself several times, the last time when he and I happened to be staying in Suffolk for the weekend with Colonel Jimmy, his half-brother. The colonel, his wife and I went to Evensong at the church down the road. When we came back we couldn't find my father anywhere. They had all the farmhands out looking for him and the villagers came in to help. Eventually they discovered him in the attic right above my bedroom – he'd taken a massive overdose of pills and

I think was heard groaning up there by someone. I must have been fifteen or sixteen, so of course, being still a child, I wasn't really told everything that was going on, but I remember my mother came down the next day by train and my father went into the Priory for treatment after that.

I think it was out of general desperation that he tried to kill himself, rather than any particular problem within his life. He must have suffered with something like manic depression, although no one ever called it that. But then, one's parents never really talked about anything serious in those days. My mother certainly had a very difficult time with him, because he would be on top of the world one moment, then down in the dumps the next.

While in the Priory – where he was for quite some time – he was given serious electroconvulsive therapy (ECT). When he came out he was fine, in that his moods were stable, but he was a totally different person. The ECT completely changed his character. I don't know if that is what invariably happened with this treatment, although I have heard of it in other cases, but the effect it had on John was rather devastating. That, again, was very difficult for my mother. He may not have been the easiest person to live with before his stay in the Priory – in fact, she always insisted that they discharged him because they couldn't deal with him – but to have a relative stranger returned to her was very upsetting and disconcerting.

My parents had married in 1940 and were a fairly dynamic couple for eighteen years. I think they had a good marriage, but definitely not an easy one. In 1959 my father left and moved in with the woman who would become my stepmother, Gwynneth Tighe, a very glamorous model whose family owned Rossanagh in Wicklow. Gwynneth became a successful TV presenter and appeared in a couple of episodes of *The Saint* as well. She was first married to Captain Nigel Knight-Bruce, an eccentric war veteran renowned for a daring escape from an Italian PoW camp in 1943, then to my father. As a stepmother, Gwynneth was lovely to me, never gave me any hassle and was very kind. I think she was very good to my father as well, but he was not an easy person to share a house with. She did eventually marry someone else, Prince Yuri Galitzine of Russia, and changed her name to Elizabeth, perhaps because it suited the title 'Princess' better. After she left him, my father, who lived on the Strand on the Green, got the props guys from the studio to create two circular blue signs, like the ones the National Trust puts up, which he mounted either side of the French windows looking onto the tow path. One said 'John Irwin lives here now', and the other said 'Princess Elizabeth slept here'. The Chiswick council wasn't very impressed and eventually forced him to take them down.

After Gwynneth, John had a terribly nice, pretty, Ugandan girlfriend, another princess – Princess Agnes – but by the end of his life he was once again being cared for by Anna, the ferocious Austrian who had been my nanny and had been with the family since 1940. She looked after him until he died in 1969 of emphysema. Anna was an extraordinary woman – terribly racist, but loyal and devoted to me. This was just as well, because although my parents were warm and loving, they were away a lot – John at work, Pippa acting – and frequently busy with other things. They were great parents to have, exciting and unusual, but they weren't at all the Walt Disney model.

2

PIPPA

My mother's background and upbringing reads like a Gothic novel – decaying family fortunes, emotional neglect, cruel beatings, even an ill-conceived trip to Africa. Born in 1918, she began life near where her mother was brought up, in Almondsbury, north of Bristol. Her maternal grandfather, Hiatt Baker, had made a fortune and established a very smart department store called Baker Baker in Bristol, rather like Brown Thomas. When Pippa's parents got married, her father Arthur (known as Tim) Stanley-Clarke, who had come out of the flying corps in 1918, was given one of the family farms by his soon-to-be father-in-law. The story goes that on the night before the wedding he went to his father-in-law and said, 'Do you think, sir, that we could possibly not have this wedding, because I don't think it will work.' To which Pippa's grandfather replied, 'Certainly not. It would be very difficult to call it off. Look at all the presents you've got.'

The next day, just before setting off for the church, Pippa's mother, Marnie, apparently rushed upstairs, grabbed a black cloak, wrapped it around herself and went to the wedding in it. So the signs and portents were not good and, indeed, it was not a happy marriage, rather it was a strange marriage, one without much in the way of love or affection. Marnie was a very clever woman apparently, on the fringes of the Bloomsbury Set, but very sarcastic and disapproving. Certainly she disapproved of giving birth to a girl. When Pippa came along she was always horrid to her, although she deeply loved Pippa's younger brother, Bino, who later won a Military Cross in Normandy in 1944 when serving with the Irish Guards.

As a child, Pippa was regularly told by her mother, 'You're so stupid, so plain, it's horrid to have to look after you.' Her nanny, a vicious woman from a farming background and of Plymouth Brethren persuasion, beat her regularly. After she was beaten, Pippa was put into a pitch-dark linen cupboard where she had to stay until she stopped crying. People were outrageous to children in those days, but even by the standards of the time, my mother's upbringing was cruel. She remembers an old man, a cowherd on the farm, saying to her once when she was older, tears pouring down his cheeks with sorrow, 'Oh, Miss Pippa, I feel so bad, I used to hear you screaming on Friday nights and I would come to the back stairs and think I'd tell that damn woman to stop it, but my courage failed me and I never did.'

Pippa's father, Tim, had a 'good war', as they said then, in the air corps, but he was a hopeless farmer. A lovely man, truly wonderful, as Pippa recalls, but with no idea how to raise pigs and cows. Her mother looked after the hens and became more and more vicious and ill and awful, while the farm lost more and more money. The livestock didn't thrive, the crops didn't grow, even the seasons seemed to be against them, until finally, when Pippa was about seven, her grandfather said to Tim, 'You've lost so much money on the farm, I'm sending you to South Africa.' And off went the family, plus a Norland nanny, with one-way tickets, on the boat to Africa.

The family lived outside Cape Town for a while, in a tin-roofed house in a beautiful village beside the sea called Hermanus, which is now a kind of Millionaire's Row. Back then, it was miles and miles of glorious sand and totally wild, where the family used to fish. Luckily the Norland nanny was a very good cook. After a couple of months, Pippa's father suddenly announced that he was going to Central Africa to shoot elephants, and off he went, not to be heard of by them again for years. Her mother's response was, 'Thank God.' She then upped the family and moved them to Pietermaritzburg because she had heard there were terribly good botanic gardens there. Indeed there were, which delighted her. The defection of her husband never seemed to bother her at all, especially while her father gave her some financial support.

By then Pippa was about eight and going to the local school. One of the other mothers stopped my grandmother one day and said, 'We really must do something for Pippa, she's so sad with her two brothers in Durban. They never come to see her and she's pining for them …' Pippa had been inventing these wonderful stories about her imaginary brothers. Her mother's response was, 'Well at least you've got an imagination. You're so stupid, but at least you have that.'

After Pietermaritzburg, Pippa's mother whipped the family off to Jeffrey's Bay to study shells, but then there was a great drama – Pippa remembers her mother crying, something she had never seen before – because there was no more money. So they had to wire grandfather, ask him for money for the return, and go back to England. The South African adventure lasted only about a year, but left a great impression on Pippa. The other significant thing was that her parents never lived together again. When her father did eventually come back into her life, he was remarried, with a second family, and his reappearance was brief and distant. I think that being abandoned by her father left a lasting hurt. She never really spoke about him. In fact, I always thought he was buried in Canada, until one day when I was staying with Pippa's half-sister, Anthea, in Essex, I wandered through the village graveyard and spotted my grandfather's name on one of the graves.

Ireland was another place that left a strong impression, because Pippa spent a great deal of time there over the years. Her mother was mad about hunting, and would take the family to Tipperary every year, to an estate called Woodruff, then owned by Major Perry. Apparently the house had been burned down at some stage of the troubles, but the owner went to London and made an impassioned speech to the Lords about how terrible it was to have nothing but a cinder to live in. He was given compensation and built a very attractive house in its place.

Zivvy Masters, daughter of Major Perry, was Marnie's great friend and famously wild. She married a Welshman who fell madly in love with her on a visit to Ireland. She went to live with him and wreaked havoc apparently, disrupting his famously grand tennis parties by cycling round and round the courts. She decided she wouldn't stay in Wales, and Pippa's mother helped her to escape back to Ireland, where she spent her days training horses and riding point-to-points.

Woodruff was a kind of beacon of civilisation in Ireland in those days, full of sophisticated, charming people, many from London, as well as the endlessly horse-mad Anglo-Irish. The novelist Molly Keane was a regular guest (Molly Skrine as she was then) – in fact, she recalled that, 'I almost lived there for six or seven years, mostly in the winter months, when I hunted three days a week on horses largely provided by Woodruff. There were so many horses in those days of the late twenties and early thirties that if you were lightweight and a moderately useful rider your fun was endless.' Molly also said, 'My mother disapproved of Woodruff – she was frightened by the idea of it. She belonged to the nineteenth century and didn't change. There was a woman there who'd been divorced and some what she would have called "dirty talk", which I didn't know a thing about, but I soon found out and was rather good at. My mother was alarmingly prudish and old-fashioned in those ways. In fact everyone there was wonderfully kind to me.'

Molly, in her turn, was wonderfully kind to Pippa. She had a vicious tongue and terrified many of their acquaintances, but she was also very amusing. It was practically the first time a grown-up had ever been nice to Pippa and they became great friends. Molly's mother was terrifying and distant too, so there was a natural affinity between them. Pippa remembers that Molly talked to her as an equal, seemed interested in her and sometimes brought her to stay with an old aunt, where they had to creep upstairs silently at night, with their candles, while huge moths flitted past their faces in the dark. And later, when Pippa became an actress, Molly did her a very good turn indeed.

Molly was a great flirt, and flirted very much with Major Perry, who owned Woodruff (Pippa recalls him as a terrible old rascal, who never did anything on the land except go out with a walking stick and slash at the heads of thistles), but her friendship with the two children of the house, Zivvy and John, was very important to her, and indirectly to Pippa, because it brought her and Molly together. John had been Pippa and Bino's tutor before they went to Africa. He was a rather bad tutor, apparently, but a very beautiful young man who got into the theatrical world in London and became friendly with Binkie Beaumont, known as the *éminence grise* of West End theatre, and one of the most successful and influential manager-producers in the West End during the middle of the twentieth century. His company, H. M. Tennent, was based at the old Globe Theatre, and put on really starry plays, often by friends of his such as Noël Coward, and controlled the West End theatres for years.

Molly collaborated with John Perry, and wrote her first play, *Spring Meeting*, which opened in the West End, directed by John Gielgud, in 1938, the same year that Molly married Bobby Keane. The play was an instant, riotous success (and well deserves a revival), with Margaret Rutherford in her first comic role. Betty Chancellor (who Orson Welles described as 'the sexiest thing that ever lived') played the part of Baby.

But then Betty got pregnant – she had started living with Denis Johnston, whom she married after he divorced Shelagh Richards – and couldn't go on playing the part, which was of a young ingénue. So Pippa got a phone call asking her to go up to London and read for it.

By then Pippa had trained at the London Theatre Studio, set up by Michel Saint-Denis, where she met all sorts of interesting people, such as Peter Ustinov and Yvonne Mitchell. It was thanks to Molly that Pippa got the call, with the blessing of John Gielgud, who was a great friend of Pippa's mother and had given Pippa her first toy theatre as a child. On the basis of the reading, she got the part. *Spring Meeting* ran for years. During the Second World War it toured, including shows in Belfast (where Pippa met my father John), and was a wonderfully reliable source of income in a very uncertain profession.

As well as *Spring Meeting*, Pippa made a couple of films, largely because she happened to walk into the right restaurant at the right time. My father usually had lunch at the Ecu de France restaurant in Jermyn Street, and one day after they were married, while walking past, she decided to pop in and see if he was there. He wasn't, but Michel Saint-Denis was, lunching with Alberto Cavalcanti, then a producer and director at Ealing Studios. Pippa joined them and was invited by Cavalcanti to take a screen test at Ealing. That got her a part in *Went The Day Well?*, written by Graham Greene, with Leslie Banks and Valerie Taylor, a classic British war film that still seems to be on television every other month.

She made a couple more films – *The Bells Go Down* and *The Halfway House* – but didn't make the transition to the really good Ealing films. She decided that, rather than appear in films that she didn't think were much cop, she would give up acting and concentrate on being a housewife and a mother. Besides, my father's career was by then very busy, which meant a lot of entertaining, going out and travelling, as well as dealing with him, which I think took up a lot of energy.

When my parents divorced, Pippa moved to the south of France with Peter Forster, her lover as she called him, and lived there for twenty-five years. Peter was a journalist who wrote for the *Spectator*, and the author of several short stories. He was, she said, very plain, but excruciatingly funny. He was a very good cook, but a bad-tempered drunk, who lunched with an air pistol at his elbow and if he saw a rat – not uncommon at the time – he would shoot it. They lived just outside St Tropez in a charming mountaintop village called La Garde Freinet. Tony Richardson, renowned film director and husband of Vanessa Redgrave, lived close by, having bought a whole mountainside. He entertained mightily. The whole of the London theatre world used to decamp there, and Pippa and Peter were constantly invited to the many parties, even though Pippa could never get on with Vanessa, who she considered a very gifted, embittered and humourless proponent of the Far Left. Thanks to these parties though, Peter and Pippa got to hang around with all sorts of interesting people, including Louis Le Brocquy, John Hockney, John Gielgud and Augustus John's eldest daughter, Poppet.

Pippa recalls being in a car with Louis Le Brocquy one afternoon, following a wild lunch party. He was drunk and driving a very powerful Bentley. Rounding a corner, the car toppled over and rolled down an embankment. Luckily it was stopped by a bush, because just below, in the shimmering Côte D'Azur heat, was a straight drop onto a motorway.

After twenty-five years, Pippa moved back from France to London without Peter, totally broke, and got a job in a joke shop in Beauchamp Place, Knightsbridge. From there, she somehow became housekeeper at New College, Oxford, even though she kept telling the new warden there, Harvey McGregor, that she couldn't cook and couldn't run a house. Her role was to entertain guests of New College and host undergraduate dinners, where she would teach them how to dress for dinner, how to eat correctly, how to sit at table and so on. So she would cook like a lunatic in her underwear, then when she was finished – she had two 'scouts' to serve the food – she would get dressed, put on her lipstick, rush in to the drawing room to welcome her guests and confide, 'I'm terribly worried about dinner because the chef's not in a good mood …'

She was there for twelve years, only retiring because Harvey McGregor had to retire. These days, she lives with us in Kildare and still, at ninety-five, has her own self-contained flat, her own friends and so on. When I think of the many changes she has been through in her life, and the cheerful, determined way she has approached them, I believe that some of her wonderful resilience must have come down to me.

3

MY EARLY YEARS

My parents were certainly exciting and glamorous, but they were distant and preoccupied too. As a result, my nanny, Anna Patscheider, was really my mother when I was very small, an utterly consistent part of my life, and such a big influence on me that I spoke Austrian dialect before I spoke English, which didn't go down terribly well in wartime Britain.

Anna arrived three weeks before I was born, from what was essentially a concentration camp on the Isle of Man. At the outbreak of the war, the British had rounded up and imprisoned all the Germans, Austrians, Italians and other enemy nationalities, and interned them on the Isle of Man. Anna had a great friend, Helena, who worked for my maternal grandmother. My mother was looking for someone to help her with the baby – me – and so they wrote a letter vouching for Anna, who came to us and stayed for the next forty years. In fact, after my parents broke up and my mother moved to the south of France, I tried to get Anna to come to Ireland with me, but she wouldn't. She stayed and looked after my father instead, and remained there until she died of a heart attack in her sixties.

Anna was a real Tyrolean peasant, strong, very direct and ferocious. She never really conquered the English language, although she used to do the *News of the World* crossword every Sunday, and sometimes even won money on it, although there can't have been two words of proper English in the whole thing.

My parents bought a big house in Buckinghamshire, where they spent hardly any time because they were both off working in London and leading their wonderful bohemian lives. I was left there alone to be brought up by Anna. My parents rarely came to visit, and there were just three of us in the house – a tiny boy, a very fierce Kerry Blue, Buster, and this ferocious Austrian woman. Anna loved gambling. Every day, as I remember it, we would walk to the village shop beside the duck pond in front of the windmill. Anna would go in and tell the postman, who was also an illegal bookmaker, to put some money on Gordon Richards, then a champion jockey. She always put something on for me too. Gordon Richards must have been like an enchanted well, because our store of money grew and grew. He was more important in my life than Father Christmas, as was Anna herself. I have no doubt the rest of the village observed us with intense suspicion, particularly at that time when stories of German spies being parachuted into the remote English countryside abounded.

Close to where we lived was a German PoW camp and three of the inmates ended up working for my parents doing gardening and maintenance work. They were very nice, with very good English, and I remember being terribly confused that 'the Enemy' seemed to be good guys. I think now that those early experiences – being brought up by Anna, making friends with the German PoWs – must have taught me something about identifying with the outsider and finding kinship with people who were different to me.

In 1949 we moved to London and I began my formal education. First there was a school in Swanage, beside the sea, when I was about six. I remember I got into trouble because I brought a white mouse and a packet of oats with me. At that school I also remember a boy being garrotted while riding a donkey. He rode straight into the clothes line and that was the end of him.

After that, I was sent to prep school – Stonehouse in Broadstairs, Kent. I was seven. Still to this day, I do not feel happy in the environs of Victoria Station, which is where The School Special departed from. There were six or seven schools in their different compartments on this train, all full of small boys wearing tweed plus-fours, waistcoats and caps. My most terrifying journey was the time when, between us, Mum and I forgot to pack a handkerchief, because I knew matron would have you beaten if you arrived back at school without one.

Broadstairs was a very frightening place. It was in a part of Kent that the Victorians had decided was very health-giving for little children, so there were eight or nine boarding prep schools and one girls' school. It was also the cabbage centre of England, growing more of that vegetable than anywhere else in the country. Before the war someone had tried to start the Channel Tunnel there, so there was a great big hole in one of the chalk cliffs. It was Ted Heath's constituency (he would later become PM), and Charles Dickens had lived there, in a house called Bleak House, looking out onto the sea, where he wrote the book of the same name. In all, it added up to a most mournful place in 1949; rationing was still in effect, there were frequent electrical blackouts, and eighty sad little boys rattled around a large, cheerless old school. We had no idea where we were and didn't have very much to eat. We relied on the masters going out and shooting pigeons and rabbits to feed us. These days I see pigeon on Patrick Guilbaud's menus for €52, which makes me laugh, although I don't often order it.

Stonehouse itself was a gaunt place. There were no curtains on the huge dormitory windows, and a lighthouse right beside us. Just off the coast was a famous sandbank, the Goodwin Sands, which was a graveyard for steamers, so it was liberally sprinkled with lightships. All night long, the light from the lighthouse would pass the windows every minute-and-a-half, while out at sea the mournful hooters of the lightships would sound. Even now I can't read Dickens' *Bleak House* or *Great Expectations* without instantly imagining myself right back there.

We were allowed to write one letter a week home to our parents, and in week six I wrote to my mother to say, 'At last I have found a feurd.' By 'feurd' I meant a friend. She still has that letter and it still makes her cry. That 'feurd' was Richard Butler, now Sir Richard Butler, from an old Anglo-Irish family and therefore even further from home than I was, who is still a friend to this day. Indeed, he was best man at my wedding to Mikaela and a constant influence and support throughout my life. Richard's career has been as a very successful international banker and, strangely, we have ended up living twenty miles from each other, with our paths crossing regularly. It is extraordinary to meet somebody at the age of seven and still be close to them so many years later.

There were a few émigré children in the school; I recall I sat next to a Polish boy called Dogilewski, who was not very well nourished, for meals. We had kippers every Friday, and I will never forget the dreadful munching sounds as he would eat the entire fish, bones and all. Then there was a very fat Greek boy, Anthony Marangos. 'Greek' and 'fat' didn't go together with the sons of the British Raj, and I think he must have had rather a hard time of it. I don't actually remember this, but it appears that I was nice to him, because years and years later he did me a very good turn. At the time I was running the Phoenix Park Racecourse and Goffs, and rather desperately looking for a high-profile sponsor for my million-pound race idea. A very good PR lady in London, Caroline Neville, introduced me to Cartier. I went into the boardroom – this was a pitch I'd given to several other companies without success – but this time, after about twenty minutes, the managing director said, 'This is an idea absolutely suited to us, we'll do it.' We did the deal – done and dusted on the spot – and walked down to the Westbury on Bruton Street, for lunch. Halfway through lunch, he said, 'Do you remember when we last met?'

I said, 'Honestly, I haven't a clue.'

'I was that little fat Greek boy you were nice to in school …'

That was how we got the Cartier Million.

My parents would try to visit me, but often it didn't work out. I'd be told, 'Your people are coming down to see you,' and I'd go and stand at the gate, waiting. Very often they didn't come, because John chickened out at the last minute; he found something more amusing to do, such as a lunch party. He was very like that. But then, so were lots of parents at the time. The idea that children should be treated gently and have their feelings considered wasn't at all popular.

4

ETON

The story of how I came to go to Eton is an unusual one. Even now, I don't fully understand it, although I am very glad it happened. Because much as people give out – rightly I'm sure – about Eton being elitist and exclusive, for me it was a wonderful experience.

Even now, there is magic to the Eton name, based on the glamour of its 600-year history, the roll-call of ex-pupils, including nineteen prime ministers, countless generals, ambassadors, colonial governors, poets such as Shelley and Swinburn, and a myriad of great actors. Eton is where George Orwell went to school, to be taught by Aldous Huxley. In *Brideshead Revisited*, it is where Sebastian Flyte and Anthony Blanche both shone as schoolboys, and where P. G. Wodehouse sent Bertie Wooster. Even Hitler was obsessed with Eton, believing it to be the perfect training ground for aristocratic paramilitaries. And perhaps he was right – more than 100 years before him, the Duke of Wellington said that the Battle of Waterloo was really won 'on the playing fields of Eton'. Beyond all the glory of the ancient stone buildings, the famous names, including future kings, the black tailcoats and acres of playing fields, the spirit of Eton is fair-minded and surprisingly egalitarian. George Orwell described it as 'a tolerant and civilised atmosphere which gives each boy a chance of developing a fair individuality'. That is what I found there.

We were not the sort of family who automatically went to Eton, at all. My mother's uncles went there, but there wasn't a tradition, even in her family, going back more than a genera-tion, and certainly my father wasn't from that kind of family. Plus, my parents wouldn't have had the money to send me under normal circumstances. My father was sometimes flush, often not, and he wasn't very good at saving money. Even now I remember the difficulties of buying my books and sports clothes for each new term.

My mother's family had money, but she didn't. And my grandmother – in a final act of spite and meanness – left all her money to the government rather than will it to my mother and uncle. I think she always regretted not being a man and therefore never 'doing her bit' in the war, so leaving her money to the government was her way of making amends to the country.

My mother saw an ad in *The Times* one day, when she was pregnant with me, saying something like 'Any lady who is now pregnant, and has a son, if she wants him to go to Eton, she can now pay £250, for his entire education.' I have still never met another person who saw this ad, or took up the offer, but my mother did. By chance, she had just been left almost exactly that sum by an old cousin, so she paid her £250, and that was my education taken care of.

There are certain prep schools whose purpose it is to stream their students for Eton. Stonehouse, while very respected, was not one of them, so I arrived there at the age of thirteen without really having a clue what to expect. Once again, Richard Butler was my only 'feud' there, although in a different house. Anna kept warning me that it was only for really rich people, but as it turned out, it didn't matter about background. I had a fair idea how to behave, but all that stuff about snobs and so on was nonsense. At Eton you never actually knew what anyone was in the outside world. You might have some idea that someone's father was a duke, like my pal William of Gloucester whose father was the Duke of Gloucester and who sadly was later to die in an air race, or even royalty, but it meant nothing – they were treated exactly the same as anyone else. As long as you were a reasonable sort of person you got on all right. If you were comic, you got on terribly well. I was reasonably good at games and always playing to the gallery, so I made lots of friends and enjoyed every single moment of it. I sent three of my sons with Mikaela – Pirate, Luke and Jago – to Eton. My fourth son, Sam Fortune, went to Bryanston because his mother and brothers didn't care for the master he had drawn, otherwise he would have gone to Eton too.

I was probably lucky, in that out of the twenty-five houses I was definitely in the oddest house, with Dr Prescot as the housemaster, where many of the forty other boys were as mad as hatters: Bugsy Kidston, Billy Dulles, Julian Ormsby-Gore, Mark Heathcote-Amory, David Morley, Charlie Hornby, Charles Millbank and many another rogue. Another close friend at that time was Grey Gowrie, later to be Minister for Arts under Margaret Thatcher; we made a couple of films together financed by my modern tutor, Giles St Aubyn, one of which won the *News Chronicle* Amateur Film of the Year Award. I learned how to use a flick knife, did a lot of acting, which I loved, and generally played the buffoon. I made friends with a boy who was half-American, who alerted us to the tsunami of remarkable music about to arrive from the United States. Truly, the late 1950s and early 1960s were incredible times to be young. Right through the 1940s and early 1950s England was grey and sad, bombed to bits, with most things still rationed and nobody creating beautiful clothes or objects. It was a nation in recovery and seriously bankrupt. Then, suddenly, in the late 1950s, this massive tidal wave arrived – Bill Haley, Little Richard, Chuck Berry – introduced to us via Voice of America and Radio Luxembourg. It really was very exciting. The non-traditionalist Etonians in my house were very attuned to this new music. Personally, my dream was to dress as a teddy boy – frock coat, thin black string tie, drainpipe trousers and brothel creepers, topped off by a Tony Curtis-style haircut that my local barber in Shepherd's Bush would style for a shilling any time before four in the afternoon.

One of my few lasting achievements at Eton was to be the catalyst in turning the so-called Eton 'Voluntary' Corps, into something truly voluntary. This Corps was the nursery for an army career – lots of drilling, running across Salisbury plain and being 'stabbed' by enemies in the middle of the night, none of which I was very good at. In fact, the adjutant thought I was more suited to the army at Agincourt than the reality of the twentieth century. My unfitness for this kind of career reached a climax the day that my year had their passing out ceremony. Someone in my house had stolen my boots and the ones I borrowed were a size too big. When an army line turns about, there is a hell of a lot of stamping and banging of boots. With all the stamping, one of my boots came right off, and we marched off down to the other end of the parade ground with one sad boot left sitting on its own. We were then inspected by the adjutant on his black stallion, and General Sir Gerald Templer, known as the Tiger of Malaya, who came up and down the lines with the cadet officer in charge and the sergeant major. I wasn't surprised when they asked where my boot was, but the army being the army, when I tried to point out the obvious to them, there was a hell of a lot of shouting from the sergeant major, who slapped my arm, whereupon my rifle was tipped onto my shoulder and clattered onto the ground. You won't be surprised to hear that he then asked me where my rifle was. That was the day I left the corps and it actually became voluntary. They finally agreed that it was a waste of time trying to teach people like me.

A lot of my friends who had been rebels when they first arrived at Eton, were, by the age of sixteen, starting to become clones of their parents. I remember saying to one of them on 4 June, which was Founder's Day, 'You go down and see if you can pick out your parents,' because the adults all looked the same. Among that sea of conformity, my parents stood out a mile. They used to visit with some of their friends from TV and film: Joan and Jackie Collins, Shirley Anne Field, a bevy of other beauties, and the hysterically funny Irish journalist, Paddy Campbell, 3rd Baron Glenavy, who made such a virtue of his stutter that he became a huge television personality in the UK. He was asked onto chat shows – he was team captain on *Call My Bluff* and a regular on *That Was The Week That Was* – and became a national treasure for his wit, charm and the fun he made of his own speech impediment. Paddy's brother Michael was a good novelist, and his mother Bea a very good painter.

My father was always very generous and would host lunch at a local restaurant in Bray, on the Thames. There would be a load of slobbering boys, and me, trying to charm the most beautiful stars every other weekend. Eton never really saw girls at all, certainly not girls like this. For a short time, I became probably the most popular boy in the school.

Everybody thinks Eton is a fairyland for homosexuals, and indeed, one of the final lectures I got from the headmaster at my prep school was about the dangers of older boys. He told me that if a big boy offered me a Mars bar and to go for a walk, I should refuse. Sadly, I was never offered a Mars bar, and I never noticed any great love affairs during my time there.

Of course nobody ever thinks of Eton without bringing up fagging; I may not have noticed any great homosexual love affairs, but fagging was a very real fact of life. Any member of the library (prefects, basically) was entitled to use the first-year boys as servants. They would regularly scream at the top of their voice 'Boy!' and as a fag, you dropped everything you were doing and ran like a lunatic. The last boy to arrive was fagged to do the prefect's bidding, whether it was picking up a suit at New & Lingwood's, or collecting his roast grouse from Rowlands.

Most importantly for me, at Eton we were treated like grown-ups, not idiotic children. Indeed, it is the ideal age to be at the equivalent of a personalised tutorial system, with far greater contact than at universities. We had so much freedom – our own rooms, with our own books – but from the age of thirteen you were expected to manage your own work, have it ready at the right time and so on. This kind of freedom was all I had ever wanted. As an only child, I spent a lot of time with my parents and their friends, doing quite grown-up things, going out to supper with various celebrities of the time and attending the theatre. Eton continued in that vein. But such self-discipline did take a bit of getting used to. For the first few years, there I was, surrounded by the best school facilities in Europe, with a library of incredible books and amazing tutors – most of whom had published learned, well-respected books – merrily wasting a world-class education.

My school reports from the time – which my mother was clever enough to keep – tell much of the story. Here is the first of them, dated 20 December 1954, and signed by my housemaster, Dr Prescot. Beautifully written, it has impeccable insights into my character and potential, and interesting, perspicacious observations on my general deportment. I don't understand why all schools can't produce reports like this one, but none, in my experience, do. I am very critical of the fact that private schools in Ireland fail dismally to take the trouble to offer parents this kind of picture of their child's development:

Dear Irwin,

Here are Jonathan's reports and marks.

I am afraid he had not been well trained to work when he arrived, and the usual thing happened. The freedom of Eton went to his head, and he thought it was a glorious place in which one sailed along at one's ease and never had to do anything disagreeable. Very soon the failures and complaints began coming in, and I had to put him in P.S. [detention, basically]. *I had already noticed that he was the brightest of the Fourth Formers in the oral unseens in Pupil Room and had the best Latin vocabulary. It was absurd that he should bring failures in his work, and still worse that the Lower Master should have to complain of his behaviour ... I am perfectly certain that Jonathan can make a success of Greek, if he wishes, and that it will be very much to his interest to continue with it. To continue means that he will be in competition with the better brains all the way up the School, and I am sure he needs that stimulus. Not altogether to my surprise Jonathan agrees with me.*

He seems to me to be a boy of exceptional vitality and very nice manners and I am rather surprised he didn't please the Lower Master, apart from his idleness. In football he was most promising, charging up with untiring energy and courage. I am sure that he has all the qualities, including the brains, to make his mark in the School, but he must discipline himself now and overcome what may otherwise spoil all his success, his ingrained tendency to carelessness.

With best wishes to you all for Christmas.

Four years later, in March 1958, my modern tutor, Giles St Aubyn, wrote to the housemaster:

Dear Prescot,

Irwin is a strange mixture of latent talent and manifest inaptitude. He is imaginative, volatile, chaotic, frivolous, enthusiastic and yet often lethargic. I first met him acting for the Film Unit and there is no doubt of his talent here. Sometimes I wonder whether he knows where his acting stops and real life begins.

His weekly exercises for me fluctuated between excellent and execrable. Most boys if they were ordered to be as untidy as possible could not with the best will in the world contrive to come anywhere near Irwin's ordinary standard of calligraphy. His best weekly exercise was a very imaginative story about circus animals which had broken out from their cage in a caravan. With the blemishes removed, this was better than similar stories of accepted authors. His worst Essays might have been written on the way between here and his tutor's.

In Private business I did a course on 'Clear Thinking'. Of all the questions I asked Irwin arising from it I do not recollect that he could answer one. This is partly due to the fact that he is unnaturally inattentive, partly due to his inability to follow any closely reasoned argument and partly I suspect due to the necessity of playing a slightly comic part to amuse the rest of the Private. In many ways he is a delightful person and in others exasperating.

Yours sincerely,

Giles St Aubyn

Also in 1958, some months later, the housemaster, Dr Prescot, in his report to my parents, had, among other things, some observations to make on my table manners:

I have noticed some very odd behaviour at Boys' Dinner – pulling his shirt in and out from his chest, to cool himself when it was hot; more or less burying his face in his hands and tumbler when drinking; pushing himself back from the table, with elbows wide apart, like a replete navvy. I wonder whether you will notice any oddities at home, or whether it is only the presence of his contemporaries that stimulates them? It is not much to worry about, but (as St Aubyn says) it might become disagreeable if continued indefinitely.

My final report from Eton, again from Dr Prescot, indicated:

Perhaps my liveliest recollections of him will be first as Mrs Radfern and then as Mrs Bare, the second Mrs Bare, in our House Plays of 1957 and 1958. I am sure his appearance as a retired and widowed barmaid, and his explanation of rejected offers – 'it was the money-bags they were after, not the old bags herself' – will be permanently engraved in the memories of those who were privileged to see him. I am so sorry neither you nor Mrs Irwin could be among them. [Obviously my parents had yet again failed to turn up.]

I shall take the liveliest interest in Jonathan's future. One way or another I am sure he will fall on his feet.

Yours sincerely,
Dr Prescot

I am still astonished at how well they caught my character and at the effort they put into considering my performance at the school.

Eton isn't a Masonic club, but you do feel totally at ease if you meet anyone from there around the world, even if they weren't in your year, because they know the rhythms of the day. However, I have met a fair number of Old Etonians who have dreadful memories of the place. When I was inviting people to one of the first lunches I organised for Old Etonians in Dublin – there are quite a few living in Ireland – at least one man shuddered when I suggested it and said he remembered those years as the worst of his life.

Looking back, I sometimes think I had the best of everything – an exciting, showbiz childhood, with the marzipan coating of Eton. If you survived – and not everyone did – that education gave you a great feeling of confidence, in every situation. My greatest mistake was to be a young buck, and very arrogant, and to use the last two years of Eton to wreak havoc and play the fool. Only towards the very end of my time there did I start to discover the excitement of learning, an interest in study and in history in particular. I did my O-levels, succeeding quite well, but Eton was very odd, and didn't encourage you to do A-levels or try for university places in those days.

Finally, I was a young Old Etonian, and therefore one of the most arrogant people in the world. When you leave Eton you know you have been moulded to be a leader. That said, I never had any illusions about going to a school above my station in life – after all, I had two actors as parents – and I knew all the way through what was expected of me, and that pay-back time came when you left and were posted to Africa or India. Because as an Etonian, this is what you were being created for – to assist in running the Empire, via the army or the civil service. I knew that my due was to the country. But it didn't quite work out like that.

Happily for me, national conscription ceased about six months before I was due my induction. And the winds of change were definitely blowing – those colonial posts that had been the natural career of Etonians, began to dry up. My generation were left with all this unexpected freedom. Instead of heading for the colonies, we arrived into the world and felt we were the natural inheritors of the New Order, something that was usually expressed by membership to exclusive nightclubs and drinking clubs in Soho.

5

TELEVISION AND TRINITY

I grew up pretty fast. I think only children do. I was also, inevitably I suppose, very at ease with grown-ups. Because of my parents' jobs and social dispositions, I went to a lot of dinners in private houses from the age of about fifteen or sixteen. I met people like Tommy Steel, Bob Monkhouse, even Eleanor Roosevelt. I remember my mother and I went sailing with her, then came back and had tea, and she was terribly nice and highly intelligent. I met a hell of a lot of people who had done well in life, and although I was the only teenager at these things, I seemed to have been gifted with something that's probably quite useless – I was good at listening and so they talked to me. They talked about themselves, the things they had done and achieved, and I learned an awful lot from that. It wasn't a formal education, but their experiences and insights gave me perspectives I suspect I wouldn't otherwise have had.

Many of these people were politicians, because of my father's involvement with *In the News*. People fought to get on that programme, because it could make or break careers. The whips used to try to influence who appeared, but my father was adamant in choosing only the most entertaining, rather than the most senior; people like Tony Wedgewood Benn, Michael Foot and Bob Boothby, who not only had a long affair with Dorothy Macmillan, wife of Harold Macmillan, but also with a young man who was a friend of Ronald Kray, one of the notorious Kray twins. The debates on the show were very deep and sophisticated, partly thanks to my father's habit of taking all the panellists out to the Ecu de France, a very good restaurant, beforehand and giving them an excellent dinner, along with a couple of bottles of wine and a brandy, before getting the limos to whisk them straight to the BBC studios where the cameras were waiting.

After the debate they usually all came back to our house and drank an enormous amount of whisky upstairs in the drawing room with my parents, while Anna entertained the chauffeurs in the kitchen. The things she learned from them about what was really happening in government were quite extraordinary!

Everything my parents did seemed glamorous, busy and exciting. Theirs was not a dull life. Perhaps because of this, even though I didn't really know what I wanted to do when I left school, I felt naturally inclined towards television. At Eton I had loved acting – it wasn't hard to be considered good there and I did show talent. But my parents reminded me of the endless years of travelling around the country, staying in forlorn B&Bs, playing in shoddy parish halls, and I got so depressed by that vision that it put me off becoming an actor. Instead, I got a few hanger-on-type jobs in light entertainment, thanks to my father. Running errands, collecting props, that kind of thing.

Then I went to work for Associated Television – ATV as it

was known – a company that had been awarded the franchise to provide programmes for the London area at weekends. This was then extended to providing weekday programmes for the Midlands area. The company was set up by two East London Jewish families, the Parnells and the Grades, in the person of Lew Grade, who was Russian Jewish and came to live in London as a child. He was Charleston champion of the world in 1926, then later went into business as a talent agent with Joe Collins, father of Jackie and Joan.

Those years taught me an awful lot about the business of show business, how to put together something so that it exuded glamour and excitement, all things that I put to very good use when I moved into the bloodstock industry. I wasn't horsey by upbringing or profession and I think it showed. Instead, I saw racing as show business. When I first began to get involved, everything was so Edwardian and fusty. In the world I stepped into, nobody would have dreamed of anything so vulgar as advertising, whereas I could clearly see the need for it. What I learned as a young man in theatre and TV really came to the fore when Vincent O'Brien asked me to run the Phoenix Park Racecourse. I saw that as pure theatre. The racing and race track were inviolate, but Vincent allowed me to entertain the crowds any other way I liked really, with things that are very old hat now but then were nearly unheard of – fire eaters, drummers, bouncy castles and the first pulled pint at any racecourse in Ireland. All of this worked splendidly, as I knew it would, and we built the crowds from 500 to over 5,000 in four years, before, sadly, the racetrack closed.

ATV had no actual studios, so instead they rented or bought old musical theatres, which were mainly very shabby by then, but retained a certain faded grandeur that was quite charming. That was a very literal example of the way in which TV was gobbling all before it and dominating the entertainment world. Anyway, I was the assistant stage manager, which basically meant tea boy, and we put on mostly rather terrible shows, but I got to meet all sorts of exciting people. I remember I worked with Diana Dors and Tommy Cooper. Once I came back early from lunch to see two men in overalls messing about on stage. In my capacity as assistant stage manager, I immediately told them to get off. It turned out they were Morecambe and Wise, already one of the biggest acts in the business.

I had come out of Eton, which has many fine things about it, but is very British Establishment – something I never made the mistake of thinking I belonged to – and here, finally, was reality. Or some sort of reality, anyway. There was one show we did, *Emergency Ward 10*, based in a hospital, rather like *Casualty*, and my job was to fill the beds with extras. We mostly used old Equity members, who were very glad of the job, such as it was, even though some of them had been quite well-known actors once. Over a cup of tea they might pull out a crumpled old bit of newspaper from their wallets, tatty old theatre notices saying 'So and so was superb as Horatio …' and show them around. It was quite heartbreaking really, to see this broken-down old fellow clinging to former glories. I was an observer – only children often are, and anyway I've always been very interested in people – so I really noticed those things, and they did prepare me to some extent for the ups and downs of life.

After I'd done my first few months in TV as the tea boy, I found the industry was very different to what I expected. I thought theatre was a bit airy-fairy and that cinema was too technical, but I believed TV would be the Steady Eddie between the two. Instead, it turned out to be full of guys with anoraks, beards and woolly sweaters. I was distraught that there didn't seem to be any other people like my father, full of energy and excitement at the possibilities. Instead, it was very bureaucratic and focused on camera angles. The directors didn't seem to have any great imagination or vision, and I just couldn't see myself as being part of that. My father had always been an outsider, and now I saw why. Instead of the brilliance and daring I had hoped for, I found good people, able people, but ultimately unimaginative. I never found a brotherhood of boys or girls my age who were really excited at what television could do, just a lot of quite dull types plodding through their relatively menial tasks. It was time for me to move on and I wasn't sorry to do so.

In my last few months at Eton, with truly dreadful timing, I had got very interested in history, and so I was looking forward to pursuing my education in Trinity College. My original plan – or rather, my parents' plan for me – had been to go to Magdalen College, Oxford. In those days, you just put your name down for whatever college your family favoured and you had a place. It was quite like an Irish political constituency in that way. But when I was fourteen, this ridiculous system was changed, quite rightly, and so suddenly Oxford was no longer an option. Instead, I chose Trinity, because I had so many wonderful memories of my times in Ireland. Apart from my childhood visits, I had also been over with my mother a lot while my grandfather and his wife were ill and dying. Dublin felt familiar and like somewhere I could settle.

Soon after I moved here, in 1959, it became even more important to me, because my parents split up and got rid of the house in London, along with most of my possessions. They just dumped everything, without really discussing it with me. My father moved to Mayfair with his mistress, who later became his wife, and my mother went with her lover to the south of France, where she bought the most beautiful *mas* up in the hills above St Tropez. However, I didn't go there very much to visit because I didn't get along with Peter, the lover.

My mother is a very kindly person, but I don't think it exercised her greatly to disappear off to the south of France. I don't suppose either of them really considered me when they made their decisions; they must have presumed that I was by then perfectly old enough to take care of myself. And so I was kind of orphaned when they broke up, and it is then that Dublin really became my home. At first I stayed with Shelagh Richards, my godmother, who lived in a place called Greenfield Manor, where UCD is now; a lovely old Georgian house split into a couple of apartments. The gardens were still there, in their original glory, and the milk arrived every morning by horse and cart. That was where I first met Edna O'Brien, who is still a great friend to this day. I went to a lecture of hers recently with my eldest daughter Lily, in Oxford, and I couldn't believe it: there were 700–800 people there and you could have heard a pin drop while she spoke.

I moved out of Shelagh's eventually, and ended up in a highly entertaining, very bohemian flat on South Anne Street, above a Chinese restaurant, opposite the Crystal Ballroom, where I lived with two actresses – Pat Leatham who was American and madly in love with Lord Kilbracken, and Nancy Manningham who was English – and a male model. Every Saturday night when the theatres closed, this flat became one of the beehives. There would be wild parties there, with people like Brendan Behan, J. P. Donleavy, Billy Quinn, John Kilbracken and Anew McMaster, showman and last of the great travelling impresarios. You could easily spot the professionals, the ones who had been before, because they always stood around the edges of the room – they knew the floors were completely rotten and highly likely to cave in, in which case they would have fallen into the Chinese restaurant below. The first-timers merrily cavorted in the middle of the room with no idea of the risk they ran.

Trinity itself wasn't up to much, in my opinion. After the wonderful tutors I had at Eton, who had really inspired my interest in history, suddenly I was back to sniggery jokes about Henry VIII's wives. I found that very disappointing. The tutorial system didn't seem to be very strong, my history tutor was very poor and Trinity at that stage was beset by an enormous number of English who had no particular affection for the place but who, like myself, had been told rather suddenly that Oxford or Cambridge wasn't an option any more and had had to find somewhere else, fast. They would have much rather been somewhere else – anywhere else – at least, that was the impression I got. Then there was a contingent from Northern Ireland who kept themselves very much to themselves, and of course a few Irish Catholics who had applied for the necessary dispensation from John Charles McQuaid, Archbishop of Dublin and Primate of Ireland. In all, neither a dynamic nor a coherent mix.

I only stayed at Trinity for nine months, but I made a lot of friends there, mainly through Players, Trinity's theatre society, which was very vibrant in those days – a lot of the people I met then went on to become renowned producers, directors and actors, such as Mike Bogdanov and Terence Brady, who was later married to Charlotte Bingham, the author of *Coronet Among the Weeds* and very popular historical fiction. Joanna Van Gyseghem, Ralph Bates, Roger Ordish and Bruce Myers all made an impact as professionals. Players was really my only intellectual outlet. Other than that I spent most of my time racing, which no other students seemed to particularly like, something that greatly surprised me because I had always thought that Ireland was uniformly horse-mad.

My life became a sort of Gingerman existence in those days: the back bar of Jammet's, Davy Byrne's, Neary's, McDaids. I was but an observer, but it was an awful lot more interesting than going into a solicitor's office or the army. In a totally different way it was even more glamorous than being a young man in London. The 1960s were very exciting times; Dublin was a bit seedy and tumbledown – they shot *The Spy Who Came in From the Cold*, with Richard Burton, in its Smithfield area, because it was more like East Germany than anywhere else they could find, and a film called *The Blue Max*, about the Second World War, where Wicklow very convincingly doubled as Flanders – but wonderfully glamorous too. You could live very well on rather little. I remember I had silk shirts made for about a fiver in a place called Tysons at the top of Grafton Street. I used to go into the Shelbourne Hotel rather often, because I'd stayed there with my parents, and say to the lovely head porter, 'Leo, I'm going to Mullingar races, I need a bit of cash.' He'd give me fifty quid and off I'd go. Then someone else took over the hotel and I breezed in one day looking for money. Instead of finding Leo, I was asked, rather sternly, 'Have you seen the credit control manager?'

I even made it into the evening papers around that time. I was staying with my godfather, Sir Edward Lindsay-Hogg, and his wife, Kathleen, for a week or two in 1961. They had a fine house on Merrion Avenue where they threw small but wild parties. The morning after one such party – which I had not attended – I awoke to the smell of a bonfire, drew back the curtains on a stunning early morning and saw a sun-drenched garden but no bonfire. Then I opened the bedroom door, only to be enveloped in a cloud of smoke. My bedroom was on a half-landing below my godfather's, but I managed to wake him and Kathleen, and get them moving down towards me. They both appeared through the smoke with towels wrapped around their hands, with Kathleen carrying a suit bag. I directed them to safety in the spare room and told them to close the door and wait while I sorted out the problem. Never wishing to look dishevelled, I quickly shaved and dressed, turned on the Kingston Trio 12-inch to raise spirits and jumped out of my window. Then I smashed the glass on the back door and crawled under the smoke till I identified the source, which was the sofa in the drawing room. I retreated to the kitchen and called 999, then waited while the operator decided whether we were a Dublin problem or a Blackrock problem; they made a speedy decision when I told them two elderly people were trapped upstairs. I went back into the garden where I found Kathleen on a window ledge holding her mink coat, while Eddie's long neck kept appearing through the smoke. At one stage (they didn't like each other very much) he handed her two ends of sheets he had tied together and told her to go first. Luckily I managed to stop that.

By then bells were ringing out on the street, so back in I went, crawled under the smoke again to the front door which I opened for the fire brigade and told them the fire was in the drawing room on the left-hand side. So they took a hatchet to the right-hand door into the dining room and smashed it to the ground before realising their mistake and turning their hoses to the drawing room. I told them of the high-risk scene developing in the spare room, from which they managed with some difficulty to effect a rescue, mink coat and all. I was delighted with photos in *Evening Mail* and *Press* and dinner with my godfather at Jammet's to celebrate.

I got about halfway through my first year in Trinity when

I was offered a job by a remarkable man, Wing Commander Tim Vigors, who had been a pilot in the battle of Britain. He was an extraordinary character whom my mother had known as a child from her hunting days in Tipperary. He ran a bloodstock agency based in Merrion Square and had also acquired the licence for Piper aircraft, one of the best makers of small aircraft, for Britain and Ireland. One day he rang my mother and said, 'I'm looking for a young apprentice, somebody who seems bright and quite honest.' She suggested me because she knew I wasn't very keen on Trinity. I had met Tim several times by then, usually at the races, and he must have formed a favourable opinion of me, because he offered me the job.

The pay was £5 a week, very little even in those days, but I took the view that getting paid at all to do what I loved doing was a tremendous thing. And I didn't really see myself as being very successful academically. My degree course was four years long, and I believed that if I came out of the sausage machine at the other end with 40,000 other people, each with a pass BA, it wasn't really going to move me on very much in the world. Whereas if I could work with this company for two, three or four years, and if I could come out with a reputation for integrity and having a bit of oomph, it would stand me better. I don't know if we had CVs in those days – I certainly didn't – but I figured I would be better off with a commercial rather than academic four years behind me. So I walked out of the back gate of Trinity with a job in my pocket and, in 1960, joined the Tim Vigors Bloodstock Agency in Merrion Square.

6

HORSES

Tim Vigors' agency trained me to do everything. I really hadn't a clue about anything very much in those days, but Tim and his partner, Tom Cooper, put me through the whole course of what I needed to know and were both huge influences on my life. The agency bought and sold horses, insured horses and shipped horses. There were just the two partners and about three of us juniors, a very small outfit, but we represented quite a lot of Americans who had mares in Ireland and we were busy.

This was my university education. You start at the bottom, doing very menial things, then gradually build up your own clientele, right from the bottom of the pile. One of the first people I bought a horse for was an old school pal. He called the horse Stop Thief and it won a few races for him, but then he went to prison a few years later, for good old-fashioned city embezzlement, and I'm not sure what happened to the horse. He wasn't by any means the first Old Etonian to go that way, and in fact I met him after he got out, in The Buttery in Dublin, and he told me prison wasn't too bad at all if you had been to public school. This sentiment was exactly echoed by Evelyn Waugh in *Decline and Fall*, when he wrote: 'Anyone who has been to an English public school will always feel comparatively at home in prison. It is the people brought up in the gay intimacy of the slums, Paul learned, who find prison so soul destroying.'

Tim was a remarkable man, a hero and larger-than-life character with an insatiable appetite for women (he seemed to leave his wives as soon as they had a baby). His family had lived at Leighlinbridge in Carlow since about the twelfth century. He was tall and broad, and I have no idea how he fitted into a Spitfire. I remember one night at the Kildare Hunt Ball, Tim became so angry with Paddy Leigh Fermor that he knocked him right across the room, where he collapsed in a corner.

Tim had the wit to recognise the importance of the American market long before anyone else and had shipped yearlings to Saratoga when no one else even knew where it was. He rented the whole of the Aer Lingus Super Constellation, a big four-engine brute, and created an office and bedrooms at the back for one return flight. He put a massive deal together involving two stallions called Nasrullah and Tulyar. That was the biggest horse deal of its time. Tim was a man ahead of his time, enormously broad in his scope of salesmanship, and a very great friend of Vincent O'Brien, who probably influenced him to look to America.

However, after a few years Tim left the company – he moved to the UK to concentrate on the Piper business, ending up in Kidlington near Oxford, where pilots are trained. Back in Ireland the company was assimilated into a very big British company, the British Bloodstock Agency (BBA), which mostly seemed to be run by old servicemen; 'colonels, captains and kings', as we used to say.

At that time the Irish horse market was rather slow and sleepy. Naturally we bred very good horses here because the land was right and the Irish are great stockmen, but we didn't have the capital to compete with the Americans, French or English when it came to buying the very best stallions, so we were rather stagnating below the top level in terms of quality. However, that all began to change in the mid-1960s. I took the view – luckily shared by some influential others – that there was an easy way to project Ireland right into the top league of horse breeding. We knew that if we could be the country with the greatest bank of high-class semen, the mares would inevitably follow, and we would become the dominant nursery. Charles Haughey was Minister for Finance at the time, and he listened to the reasoning of our team, led by Captain Tim Rogers and John Byrne. In 1969 Haughey reformed the Finance Act in such a way that anyone who wanted could put their money into a stallion share and the income they earned would be exempt from taxation; very simple and very effective. Within five years the quality of our stallions had improved immeasurably. Suddenly a lot of city money started coming into the industry. The more go-ahead of our breeders were able to attract their friends in and join syndicates, which meant they could afford the very best that was on offer in breeding terms. That is basically how we went from being just a good breeding country with pretty everyday stallions, to having the finest bunch of stallions available in Europe.

That incentive changed the Irish thoroughbred industry for ever and I am still very proud to have played a part in it. In fact, the idea was so successful that I later morphed it into the Irish Stallion Incentive Scheme, which took some of the additional cash the stallion owners now had and passed it on to the brood mare owners, because I felt that Haughey's innovation should benefit the entire industry and not just one section of it. With the extra cash, successful brood mare owners were also rewarded, meaning they too could improve stock, and the net result was better horses all round. The Irish Stallion Incentive Scheme then morphed into the European Breeders' Fund, to this day the largest pan-European sponsor of racing.

I always thought it was a pity that the incentive given to writers and artists in the same act wasn't followed through in its original form. Initially, part of the deal was that those bene-fiting (the writers and artists) would agree to give a certain number of hours of lectures a year to the university of their choice. That would have had a definite, wonderful effect on the culture of the country, I'm sure, but nobody enforced it and it fell between the sheets.

In 1965 I set up the *Irish Horseman* magazine, to promote the Irish horse. I couldn't believe there were magazines for sailing and for flying, but no glossy magazine for the horse industry. I started it with two pals, using my flat in Fitzwilliam Square as offices, and we put in £33 each, £100 in total. Maymes O'Reilly wrote the show-jumping side, I wrote the other side and bullied a few racing journalists to write for me, for about £5 an article. We had great fun pasting it up on the floor of my flat, and eventually sold it for a profit to the *Farmers Journal*.

Towards the end of the 1960s there seemed to be a stirring from Japan to create a thoroughbred industry, as their Ministry of Agriculture seemed to wish to move people away from the production of rice into more high-value, high-employment areas of agriculture. They started to buy Irish and European horses through the BBA, but the 'colonels, captains and kings' of the BBA didn't care for the Japanese at all: the Second World War was still a very recent memory – and so the straw was handed to me. Quite extraordinarily, the green shoots of the Japanese market became a volcano, as strong as the Arab market is now. There I was, stuck in the middle of it in my mid-twenties, travelling the world, bidding extraordinary sums in the marketplaces of America, Australia and Europe on the top horses. Not that the money was mine, obviously. I just got my salary, which was still quite modest – but the lavish lifestyle was on expenses. Essentially somebody else was paying for me to travel around the world, stopping off wherever I liked. In those days aeroplane tickets were far more flexible than they are now, so I got to explore the Philippines, where I became great friends of the Cojuangcos, one of the ruling families, and India, where I was lucky enough to buy a horse called Everyday for under £1,000, for Rajendra Singh of the Doaba Stud. Everyday was to become India's champion stallion for many years and returned the Singh family financially to the position they had enjoyed before Independence.

As a director of the BBA, I headed up the Japanese market

for about twelve years, as it steadily became more and more vibrant. It still is fairly vibrant; the Japanese are definitely players in the marketplace, but they have been thoroughly superseded by the Arab market now. The Japanese have bred some good horses, but, with the exception of one or two families, it is still a very parochial scene there. Up to a few years ago you weren't allowed to ride in Japan as a foreign jockey, or train horses there as a foreign trainer, which naturally inhibits any real dynamism. Certainly in those days, and still probably today, you wouldn't really be in a rush to tell smart Japanese friends that you were coming to their country for the horse racing. It is perhaps the only country where racing is not seen as the 'sport of kings'.

Despite the notoriously subtle but inflexible rigours of Japanese society, where one ignorant move can lead you to unintentionally but profoundly insult someone, we had no lessons in protocol prior to our trips there. We were just chucked in at the deep end. Our travelling party was made up of a partner from the London office of the BBA, a partner from the French office, myself from the Dublin office and sometimes an American, so that we were able to give the Japanese a whole overview and access to all the major horse markets.

The Japanese didn't particularly like coming to Ireland. We didn't have any cabarets or brothels, and they disliked our food (and it was hard to blame them in those days, especially when you saw the endless plates of coronation chicken they were forced to eat in country hotels). We didn't even have the kinds of cars they were used to – just a fleet of ancient Austin Princesses, awful funereal things. On one trip we had two of these; the interpreter and I were in one and a bunch of Japanese clients, who seemed to be always asleep, in the other. We finished our business and brought them back into Dublin around 5 p.m., to a giant Chinese restaurant on George's Street, where we fed them. At about 6.45 p.m. we had all finished eating and we Irish were all ready to call it a night, when the interpreter came up to me and said, 'Mr Irwin, Mr Tamashima want to go dancey-dancey.' Well, I didn't know what we were going to do. So I asked our chauffeur, John Wright, the guy we always used, 'Where does one go dancey-dancey in Dublin?' With great inspiration, we took them down to Cleary's ballroom, paid two shillings and sixpence for each of them to get in, and left them doing the Paul Jones. This presumably wasn't what they had in mind at all, but the next morning the interpreter said it had been their best night out in Europe ever.

My life ticked over like this for a good while – plenty of international travel, a steady advancement in my career, creative improvements to the Irish bloodstock industry – and it was all very pleasant. The BBA were the largest managers of stallions in Ireland, and working there was just like dealing with stocks and shares. We moved to bigger offices in Lansdowne Road and took on more shipping, more insurance, and did very well. Then, in 1974, the Royal Dublin Society (RDS) sold off its thoroughbred sales grounds, the paddocks as they were called, and that changed everything. These were the only sales grounds in the country, located where the Allied Irish Bank Centre is now, opposite the RDS. They were very sophisticated, with 400–500 loose boxes. Robert J. Goff, the only thoroughbred auction house in the country, had by then leased them for eighty years. CIÉ had even put in a special rail link to Ballsbridge for the sales, and then the RDS sold them to the bank for £4 million without telling anybody: not a single word to the resident tenants, no consultation process, no opportunity for Goffs to come up with an alternative bid. Overnight, the physical hub of the entire industry was wiped out. A very dark day in the history of the RDS.

As a result, around 60 per cent of the top Irish horses for sale went to England – to Tattersalls in Newmarket, Suffolk – so this was now a real blow to the Irish horse market. Our chances of competing with the UK were suddenly smashed. The RDS wasn't prepared to build a sales ring anywhere else on its grounds, and none of their suggested solutions was acceptable to Goffs or the members of the Irish Bloodstock Breeders' Association.

Meanwhile, at the same time, the international horse market was pretty depressed, and Goffs found itself on the verge of bankruptcy. Bad times for the industry – no sales grounds and nearly no auctioneers. There was a very good chance that Ireland was about to finally lose any chance of selling its own horses. I was determined that wouldn't happen. I had long been convinced of the need for a robust national industry – it was to promote that very thing that I had started the *Irish Horseman* – instead of always being some kind of poor relation to the British industry. We were doing so well in many ways, thanks in great part to the Irish Stallion Incentive Scheme, and I couldn't countenance that we would have success whisked away from us now. After all, this was one of our major agricultural industries.

To me it was simply not acceptable that Irish horses should be sold by one of our main marketing rivals. That's not being anti-English – it's just a realisation that you lose your own brand straight away if that happens. If you're a New Zealander and you buy a horse in Suffolk, you think that horse is English, no matter where it was bred. That fundamental reality is what drove me. I found it deeply shocking that Ireland was – and is – the only thoroughbred nursery to sell the majority of its best horses in another country. One example of the disparity between the countries was that, in the form book that embraced both England and Ireland, an Irish-trained winner would be noted as 'trained abroad', no name, no details. It wasn't until Paddy Prendergast became the champion English trainer of his age that they finally acknowledged Ireland and the winner would read 'trained in Ireland by —'. Until then, we were locked out, treated like poor colonial cousins.

Nobody else seemed very much fussed by what was happening though. I was on the council of the Irish Bloodstock Breeders' Association by then, and I do remember getting up and saying, 'This simply can't go on any longer, and if it makes any difference to anybody in this room, I'm prepared to give up my partnership in the BBA [I'd been made a partner quite young] and go out and put a syndicate together. Despite my accent, I believe the Irish should be able to sell their horses in Ireland.' The breeders all said, 'That would be a very nice idea …', mainly I think because it meant they wouldn't have to do anything more about it.

Goffs at the time was owned by the Myerscough family

(who owned Coyle Hamilton insurance company), the Ganleys and the Loves. Joe McGrath, of the wealthy McGrath dynasty, happened to be on the board. His brother Paddy, chairman of Waterford Glass and the Irish Hospital Sweepstakes, was not prepared to see his brother on the board of a failing company. So he approached me to see if I would indeed put together a syndicate, with his support, and create a new Goffs. One of the most positive moves was that Robert Myerscough had taken an option on 74.6 acres of land in Kill, County Kildare, where Goffs is now. Like him, I took the view that moving was a very good idea. As the various negotiations continued, it had become very clear to me that we could not return to the RDS and be beholden to the same landlords as in the past, with no security of tenure. I believed we should build our own sales pavilion, and be owners, not tenants. However, the question of money was paramount. I was on my way to raising the £1.8 million needed privately, but the Irish breeders insisted they had to become shareholders. In the end, their contribution was fairly pathetic, just £160,000, and it cost us more than that to bring the company onto the stock exchange.

I had done a lot of work over the years with an auctioneering company in America, Fasig-Tipton USA, and their managing partner John Finney was a great friend. He agreed to come in on the plan and after that it wasn't too hard to interest other investors – Walter Haffner, who owned Moyglare Stud, and Dr Schnapka, a German who owned Ferrans Stud in Kilcock. Captain Tim Rogers of Airlie and Grangewilliam Studs came on board, as did Robert Sangster.

So we got our money and started to build like little moles. A great friend of mine, Niall Scott, of Scott Tallon Walker, came in as our architect, and we planned what was to be the first purpose-built bloodstock sales complex in the world. We travelled to Australia, America and England looking at other sales grounds and incorporating elements of what they did best into our design. We created a glorious structure of concrete and glass, reached by an underpass that funnelled off from the dual carriageway, then up and into Goffs. The underpass cost us £27,000, and was later sold to the NRA (National Roads Association) for £4 million; it is blocked off now.

However, I didn't want merely the most modern and best-equipped sales complex, I also wanted a whole new approach to doing business within the horse industry, and I thought that this was the time to get that. I was mortified that class distinction was still so rampant; it was difficult for an outsider to learn even how to buy a horse at a sale in those days, and the idea that anyone would actively seek to attract younger people was a joke. Tattersalls, our great rivals and the longest-established auctioneers, whose sales ring was opposite Harrods in London until after the Second World War, had an ex-directory phone number that wasn't even on their writing paper, which to me said it all: 'Hawkers round the back' basically. There was no way of contacting them if you weren't already 'in the know', which meant the industry was an entirely closed shop. That always struck me as patently ridiculous, and I resolved that my door and the doors of Goffs would always be open to anyone who cared to come.

I remember after we finished building Goffs, the charming then-managing director of Tattersalls took me out to lunch and said, over pudding, 'Now, Irwin, you won't try and steal any of our clients, will you?'

'I've spent a million and a half getting this complex built; I will rather be obliged to get all the clients I can.'

'Oh. That's a bit upsetting,' he replied.

Halfway through the build – for which we had given ourselves a very tight deadline because it had to be open for the advertised autumn sales – the RDS decided that actually it was going to build a new sales pavilion after all, where the Simmonscourt extension is now. It had realised belatedly, that, when times were good for the horse market, the Goffs cheque was probably the largest one it received all year, so it decided to get back into the game. Given that it got an awful lot of money for selling the original sales grounds – £4 million – what it should have done was sit back and design the best international conference centre known to mankind. Instead, because it so badly wanted to hold a sale before we did, it rushed up an awful barn-like construction that to date has never functioned as well as it should.

Bad as that site was, it did us a lot of damage. The sales complex never divided the top end of the market – we held on to that very successfully – but it did hurt. After a year or two, the RDS sales company went bust and the grounds were sold again, this time, to our horror, to Tattersalls. This was the greatest betrayal since Dermot MacMurrough asked the Normans to come over and help him in his battle against the local chieftains. We now had the enemy within our own fences. Tattersalls moved location quite quickly, because they too realised the building was awful, but getting into the RDS gave them an opportunity to establish their toe-hold, something that could only mean trouble for us.

In fact, everybody thought we'd go out of business straight away, but we didn't. We got the sales pavilion built on time and managed to grow the rich end of the market, which was flat racing. We were all young and enthusiastic at a time when youth was scarcely appreciated in this country. Everything commercial seemed to be in the hands of old people who decried us because I was the oldest, at thirty-four, and the average age of the Goffs executives was twenty-nine. That again was very exciting, because it felt fresh and new. However, I was married with children by this time, and the stress of raising the money and getting Goffs built and open on time, to such a tight deadline, undoubtedly had a knock-on effect at home.

7

ENTER MIKAELA

To go back in time: Horse Show week of 1961 and my life was about to change significantly. I got a call from a society lady I knew of, Mrs Penny Kavanagh, wife of Mont Kavanagh who had created Hardwickes, a family business that became one of the most successful property companies in Ireland. She said she believed I was dining that evening with Donald and Mary Davies, in their stunning house, Charleville, outside Enniskerry, and that her niece from Rome had also been asked, but she had no transport. Mrs Kavanagh – who seemed to know everything – believed I was also a guest at the Spanish Embassy for cocktails earlier in the evening, which I was, and so was her niece. 'Would you mind very much giving my niece, whose name is Mikaela, a lift?' I said of course I wouldn't mind.

Secretly, I was thinking, 'Jaysus, here we are halfway through Horse Show week, and suddenly along comes a niece from Rome and no one else seems to want to give her a lift. This must be the fattest, plainest niece you ever saw in your life!' So anyway, charitable little Johnny goes to the Spanish Embassy and is at some point introduced to Mikaela Rawlinson, who blows his socks off, because she is simply the most beautiful girl he's ever seen. Absolutely amazing. Glorious red hair, freckles, green eyes, with a fascinating, mercurial character and intellect: full of natural wit and vivacity.

Mikaela's father, Sir Peter Rawlinson, was an English barrister, author and politician, who became attorney-general under Edward Heath. He had married her mother, Haidee Kavanagh, Penny's sister-in-law, who had been brought up in Killiney. Peter's true ambition was to have been appointed lord chancellor – as seemed very likely during the 1970s – in which case he would have been the first Catholic to hold the office since Thomas More in 1532. That didn't happen (Thatcher blocked it) but he did, as solicitor-general, act for the crown in the Profumo Affair and later cross-examined Delours and Marian Price after the Old Bailey bombing. Mikaela adored him, and I admired him greatly. Plus I loved the fact that, as MP for Epsom and Ewell, he got a permanent box at the Epsom racecourse.

After that marriage ended, Haidee married a very lovely, gentle Canadian man, Charles Turner, who was a Turner of Turner & Newall Asbestos Co. They lived a wonderful life in Rome, where Mikaela was mostly brought up. By the time I met her she was working as a model with Carosa, one of the big fashion houses, and was very much a part of the smartest Roman society.

As far as I remember, Mikaela took no notice of me at all that first night at the Davies', but somehow we stayed in touch. During my third year with the Tim Vigors Bloodstock Agency, the senior partner told me, 'We're sending you for work experience either to a German racing stable or a stud farm in Rome.' Now, I couldn't say, 'Please send me to Rome because that's where Mikaela is,' but I think fate intervened because, without me pushing at all, I ended up being sent as a stable lad for four months to Scuderia Olgiata, which was about fifteen miles outside Rome.

I rang Mikaela and told her, and she said, 'Oh, my parents will be delighted.' They must have been quite pleased, because once I got to Rome, Haidee invited me out every single day. They had a beautiful villa on the Appia Antica, which was full of wonderful paintings and *objets d'art*, and Haidee and Charles were terribly kind to me.

I had driven down to Rome from Ireland in my British racing-green Triumph TR4, and every evening I would drive into Rome and meet Mikaela in a bar on the Via Condotti. It was becoming a romance at this stage, even though I still could not believe that this beautiful girl wanted to spend time with me. And then Mikaela asked me to what is probably the smartest ball in the social calendar, the Paris-Rome Ball, with dinner beforehand at her family's villa. The dinner party and ball were white tie, which I, in my role as a stable lad, had unfortunately not brought with me. But Mikaela very kindly said that she would organise it for me, and that if I got out early, I could dress at the house. Which I did, duly arriving and being shown to one of the spare rooms to get changed.

The smell as I unpacked this tail suit was appalling. Sweat, moth-balls, damp, maybe a touch of mould. I put on the white shirt, which was fine, but the shirt front was plastic and kept flipping up into my face. Unfortunately the clip-on white bow tie was 13.5-inch size, and the collar was 15 inches, so there was a terrible bulge at various points around my neck. The suit was also too big, so the tails came down to my ankles. And I stank like a polecat. As the horrors of the suit unfolded, I thought, 'Where does this thing come from?' It turned out it came from a theatrical costumier, Cavalieri, who had an office round the corner from the villa. I'd say it had travelled the length of Europe – anyone who ever played a hero, villain or drunken butler in Roman repertory had sweated into it under the footlights. Mikaela had simply sent someone off to find a tail suit, and this is what came back. The first time she actually saw it was when I appeared in it that night.

I walked out onto the elegant patio, with these really grand continentals, all with titles, all incredibly well-educated and sophisticated. Here was I, a smelly little man with a shirt front that kept flipping up. The dinner party was composed of smart young men from Paris society wearing blue cornflowers in their lapels, and smart young men from Roman society, plus beautiful girls, including Mikaela and her sister Dariel. By what seemed a general consensus, I was sort of ignored. I was now the kind of ugly, unwashed hanger-on, as I had so wrongly once imagined Mikaela to be.

We got through dinner somehow, although neither of the girls on either side of me seemed terribly interested in my conversation. Then we set off for the ball, which was in the most beautiful Roman palace, with a long flight of marble steps up to the front doors, footmen in white uniform holding flaming torches on each step, and the cream of Parisian and French society ascending. And *moi*. I looked like Max the Mouse. Every third step, my heel would catch in the over-long tails, and I'd lurch a bit, then stagger up the next step.

The ball was not a great success, for me anyway. It's hard to shine as Max the Mouse, so I sat around looking miserable. Eventually a limo was very kindly provided at around 3 a.m. to return me to my little room in Olgiata. I went to bed about 5 a.m., and since we had to get up at 5.30, I didn't change, just flopped on the bed, still in my stinking tail suit. Half an hour later, I got up. The stable manager – a terrifying man – hadn't arrived in the yard, luckily, so the other lads and I put out all the mares and foals, everyone laughing at me like drains because I was still in my evening clothes. Then we mucked out all the boxes. The mangers were huge, old-fashioned wooden troughs, filled with sweet-smelling cut grass. When I had finished the boxes, I nipped into one for a snooze and woke up about an hour later with the fearsome stable manager standing over me with a pitch-fork. It was like the nativity scene gone very, very wrong, with a grown-up baby Jesus much the worse for wear.

The romance with Mikaela didn't falter despite this and the fact that I wasn't a great catch. I came back to Ireland after my four months were up, but we continued to ring each other. That summer I drove down to visit my mother in the south of France, then went on to Rome to collect Mikaela. We went to Naples together and then to Capri, where her mother and stepfather had a beautiful house and a yacht.

We got engaged and were married on 22 February 1964. Because Mikaela's surrogate home was with the Kavanaghs in Clonsilla where I worked, the natural thing would have been to get married in Dublin. But that gorgeous man John Charles McQuaid banned it because it was a mixed marriage – I was Protestant, Mikaela was Catholic – so we ended up being married in Cheyne Walk in London, by Father De Zulueta, an intellectual. We had a personal telegram from the Pope, which would surely have driven McQuaid quite mad.

It was remarkable really that Mikaela came to live here. Until moving here, she had lived a very exotic but slightly gypsy-like life – between smart finishing schools in Geneva, the south of France, Rome and Capri. She was one of the most attractive and sought-after girls in Roman society and really could have done anything she wanted with her life. However, Ireland did have a strong prior claim on her. She spent a lot of time here with her grandmother until she was twelve or thirteen, at Holy Child School in Killiney, before the move to Rome, so that coming here with me wasn't a complete step into the unknown. All the same, I'm sure it was very lonely, initially anyway, because although she did have relations, she didn't have many friends. She wanted to work, but there wasn't really much going for someone like her. She did a couple of months in PR for Switzers department store, but found it fairly deathly. After that, she concentrated on the children – about a year and a half after we were married, Pirate was born, followed by Luke, Jago Michael Patrick and finally Samson Fortune.

At least I was able to find us somewhere decent to live,

though mostly by chance. I had a great friend, Mervyn Wing-field, grandson of Lord Powerscourt, and one day over lunch he said, 'I've got this apartment in Dublin; I don't need it any more.' It was a lovely duplex apartment at No. 10 Fitzwilliam Square, so that's where we moved. We had a Great Dane, who couldn't go up and down so many stairs, so he had to be carried, which was all right when he was a puppy, but not great when he became a full-grown dog. For a time, when he was small, we had a laundry basket on a rope, and we used to lower him to the street so he could do whatever he needed, then haul him back up again. It worked perfectly.

I think I was on something like £30 a week in those days. Poor Mikaela was stuck in Dublin, with a husband on a mediocre income, but who was trying very hard to prove himself and therefore working long hours and travelling often. It can't have been easy for her, but we did have a riotous time and some interesting guests. The flat became an eclectic transient camp for actors, musicians, the odd well-bred ex-inmate of Wormwood Scrubs, and even Eleanor Philby on the way to join her husband, Kim, in Moscow. I remember her as rather dowdy and dreary, though in retrospect I realise it can't have been an easy time for her.

One Christmas we were in London and went to a party my father gave in his house at Strand on the Green, which became wilder and wilder. Stupidly, my father offered £500 to anyone who could swim the width of the Thames. As only a lunatic would have considered such a thing, we thought no more of it till we heard a roar from the far bank, and realised a great friend of his, an intrepid horseman and musician, Gay Kindersley, son of Oonagh Guinness by her first husband Philip Kindersley, was on the far side, and was coming back to claim the £500. Despite everyone screaming at him to stay where he was, Gay dived back in, and got into difficulties midstream. I went in after him, quickly followed by an Etonian pal, now the renowned actor Jeremy Clyde. The water was icy, it was pitch black and Gay was now in real trouble, made worse by swimming into a gaggle of moored boats, under which he was being dragged. By the grace of God, we found him and dragged him to safety, only then realising what danger we had all been in. To his credit, my dad coughed up the £500, which was then split three ways.

Irish society still had the same lovely openness that I had found in my Trinity days; in fact, I used to think it was like Jack Russell puppies in a basket, everything merrily turning and churning around. All sorts of interesting people came here, and there were great parties given. Aileen Plunkett, one of the three Golden Guinness sisters, who lived in Luttrellstown Castle and had been married to Brinsley Plunkett, was a fabulous hostess who gave magnificent dinner parties. These started quite formally – a round table which seated thirty or forty people, footmen in white gloves, beautiful flowers, everything perfectly arranged and smelling wonderful – but often ended very late, in the basement nightclub. Over the years we met Hubert Givenchy, the fashion designer, there, also Prince Rainier and Princess Grace of Monaco, the Rolling Stones, Vincent Poklewski-Koziell, Charlie Haughey, Norah

Fitzgerald, Frankie Svedjar and Michael Morris, 3rd Baron Killanin – soon to be president of the Olympic Council. Aileen loved entertaining, and had a very mischievous sense of humour – sometimes she'd put a bowl of fake vomit beside guests' beds, or a stuffed dummy between their sheets – which meant invitations from her, which seemed to come every three or four months, were quite an event.

Luggala, the Wicklow estate of Aileen's sister Oonagh, was another interesting scene. Oonagh had famously eclectic taste in people, happily mixing her aristocratic friends with writers, painters, poets, even IRA men, in parties that sometimes went on for days. People would come for dinner, then emerge, blinking, several days later, unaware quite how much time had passed. My friend Grey Gowrie once went for a weekend, and ended up staying three weeks. 'I'm not really a drinker, but I think I was tight most of the time,' he later said. Brendan Behan, who went as often as he could, said the only rule was not to be tedious: 'You may say whatever you like, so long [as] you don't take too long about it and it's said wittily.'

This is also where I met Tara Browne, one of the most fascinating people I have known. He was about fourteen when I first met him, during my Trinity days, at a party at Luggala. He and Garech, his elder brother, were both seated at the table with us, and I remember being dumbfounded that both had a full bottle of Irish whiskey at their place. Tara was probably the most beautiful person you've ever seen in your entire life – unbelievably good-looking and very attractive to be around, amazingly gifted in conversation. When he was killed in 1966 a big light went out. He was one of the good people I met in my life, and his loss was terrible.

In those days, most of the country houses were in financial difficulty and beginning to be under-staffed, but the Guinness houses were still wall-to-wall footmen in white gloves. Desmond and Mariga Guinness, in Leixlip Castle, entertained a lot of intellectuals – professors from Trinity and American academics. Mariga once said, 'Ireland is heaven, everyone is so dotty and delicious and no one dreams of taking anything seriously, except, perhaps the Horse Show,' which is rather what I thought about it myself.

Mikaela and I also entertained, particularly around the Goffs sales weeks, when we would have international buyers to stay, but really Mikaela wasn't that interested in horses. She loved going to Ascot, but the actual chat about pedigrees and fetlocks and withers bored her. She rode and hunted while living in Italy, but mostly gave that up when she moved here. And I know the contrast between Rome, so very sophisticated and glamorous, and the horsey circles here in Ireland, where rules like wearing a hat and gloves to the races were rigidly enforced, wasn't a flattering one. She said it was like stepping back into the 1940s or 1950s, which was probably not a good thing. Horse people are very at ease within their own community, but they don't read very much and have very few interests outside horses.

In about 1967 we moved from Fitzwilliam Square to a Queen Anne house on the main street of Leixlip that we bought for a few hundred pounds. We ended up selling it to the Church of Ireland, because the bishoprics of Meath and

Kildare were being combined and they needed to find a home for a bishop in the right place. Mikaela probably has one of the best interior decorating eyes I've ever seen, and what she could do to a house was remarkable.

After that, we moved to a house that became Moyglare Manor Hotel, in Maynooth; a giant rundown Georgian house that we bought for almost nothing, because it came with about 700 acres, and I was able to find two other people to buy the land. One part became the Moyglare Stud Farm, while the other was sold to a large cattle farmer and estate agent. They took the land, we got the house and about twelve acres. The house dated from about 1790, and was very fine, but very tumbledown. The first night we were there a ceiling fell in and we did wonder why we had bought it. But Mikaela worked her charm and spell on it, and it became one of the most stunning houses in Ireland. She did it up so beautifully, with a wonderful team of local builders, and we eventually sold it for an absolute fortune, but I think that indirectly led to our divorce.

Divorce is a nightmare, a contest no one ever wins, and after twenty-three years together, it was pretty bloody stupid. I do know that I have had the most incredible life in so many ways, but sometimes it has been scary and terribly sad too. The failure of the marriage – my failure – was dreadful, and upset the children terribly. I would still count Mikaela among my great friends, someone I admire enormously, but those were difficult days.

Mikaela was having our last baby, Sam Fortune, in London. I had gone over to see them, and was now back, and she rang one night and said, 'How's everything?' I said, 'Oh, it's great; I've sold the house.' Now, the house wasn't even on the market, but a very good local house agent had rung one day and said, 'I've got some people who'd love to see the house.' That did happen from time to time since there was a hall with rather famous plasterwork, so people would sometimes ring up and ask to stop by. I said, 'That's fine,' and I wasn't even there when they came. Anyway, the agent rang back, and asked, 'Would you ever consider selling the house?' I said, 'Of course not; don't be ridiculous,' but he kept ringing back, with higher and higher offers, and in the end the numbers became very appealing indeed. Eventually, I agreed the sale for really crazy money.

Now, I definitely did it the wrong way round. I should have had the manners to talk to Mikaela first, but I thought she wouldn't be able to believe the money we'd got for the house and that she would be pleased. She wasn't a bit pleased, of course. In fact, she got very upset, and I don't blame her. There she was in London, with a newborn baby, looking forward to going home, and suddenly home was not there. It was not a good move on my part and I do think that was the beginning of the crumbling of the partnership.

Shortly afterwards her mother, Haidee, died in London. Such a mesmerising woman – a mixture of class and wit – I adored her, as did Mikaela. I think her death caused Mikaela enormous distress.

After leaving Moyglare, we moved into the most beautiful house, Sandymount, that we bought from Grey Gowrie, my old school friend, and we were there for about eight years. Again

Mikaela worked her magic on the house and gardens, but the atmosphere was tense, and I think we were both very lonely in our own ways. I was very taken up with work and away a lot, travelling. Getting the new Goffs built in nine months was horrifically stressful because we had the autumn sale booked in, so we couldn't be a single day late. I'm sure that didn't help me to be a considerate and attentive husband.

I know it ended in failure on my part, but the marriage was a very positive part of my life. Mikaela raised our four boys superbly, she saw me rise up in the BBA and become a partner, and begin working at Goffs. Together we had wonderful times and I cannot speak too highly of her. We still talk nearly every day, although she now lives in England, and I admire her enormously for the strength she has shown through everything, particularly the death of our beloved son, Sam Fortune, just after he left Bryanston.

When the divorce finally came, we sold Sandymount to Ronnie Wood, the Rolling Stone, who still owns it and has a stud farm down there. His manager, Nick Cowan, was a great friend of mine from Eton, which is how the meeting came about, and Ronnie was a real pleasure to deal with. We sat in the kitchen in Sandymount one night and probably had two bottles of vodka between us, and at about six o'clock in the morning we did the deal.

8

GOFFS, SHERGAR AND THE CARTIER MILLION

The Irish horse has long been well known internationally; my old boss and mentor Tim Vigors had successfully developed the American market for European horses, and within that Ireland was no slouch. But there was room for more, and with Goffs I wanted to really market Irish horses internationally, as a brand in themselves for the first time. My plan was to bring Irish breeders, selling Irish horses in Ireland to an international audience.

The stress of getting Goffs built on time was huge, but we did it. We opened not a day late and not a penny over budget in time for the yearling sale of 1975. That opening sale had a dramatic effect on the whole market, largely because we approached auctioneering in a very different way. Until then, auctioneering of horses in Europe had been more like basic bid-taking, a fairly sedate and subdued affair. I brought what I'd learned in America back to Ireland and we changed all that. We wanted to be sexy and innovative, in an area of business that had lacked any innovation for hundreds of years. The team – David Nagle, Philip Myerscough, Charlie Murless and Alan

Cooper – were all young, dynamic and hard-working. We knew we could do this and that the time was right to blow the musty old world of bloodstock sales wide open.

We had no windows in the auditorium because I didn't want people looking at the beautiful countryside; I wanted them looking only at the rostrum. I restricted the number of people who could ever get on the rostrum – leaving just the spotter, the auctioneer and a clerk to take down the bids – because any more takes away from the theatre of the event and the importance of the auctioneer. I played everything as if this were indeed a stage. There were spotters around the ring, ready to shout out when anyone made a bid – something never seen in Europe before. For the important evening sales, all our male staff wore black tie, because I believed that enhanced the atmosphere and the dreams. And the dream, of course, is that you will buy a horse with that particular touch of magic that will go on to win the Derby and stamp itself into the public consciousness in the way that only a very few special horses do, and maybe even put you on the cover of *Newsweek*.

The Goffs yearling sale was the key income driver of the company and it was organised in three tiers: Invitational was the highest end and that was limited to the really top horses. After that came Premier, which was the bulk of the sale, followed by Sportsman, which was run on the last day of the sale and included sound horses from the lower commercial spectrum.

Nobody now will remember the birth of the international bid board that is common within auction houses around the world. In fact, it was invented by us and spread around the world when my very good friend Peter Wilson, chairman of Sotheby's, came to one of my sales and couldn't believe what he saw. Our bid board showed the price in yen, dollars and sterling. As the bids went up, they would be simultaneously converted and displayed. That too added to the theatre, the drama of what was unfolding. What we were doing was still Irish, but there were definitely a lot of overtones of *Tom and Jerry* to it too!

And each night, after the sales were finished, we would have parties upstairs in the restaurant, which we made sure stocked the very best wine and food. That was as important as all the other details; if we were to attract international buyers to Goffs, we needed to make sure we could keep them happy once we got them here. Customer care was a major part of our plans. I was a showman – I admit that frankly. My days in front of the footlights in Eton and working with the best of London East End entertainers paid off. And that was an aspect of my team I was keen to develop: I encouraged the young men I had found running Goffs when I first arrived – David Nagle, Philip Myerscough and Peter Murray – to play to the gallery a bit.

We also diversified, starting up within Goffs an insurance company, a finance company and a real estate sales company. To spread the brand name Goffs, and to encircle Tattersalls, we opened Goffs France, in Deauville, which now, under the name Arqana, has the monopoly of thoroughbreds and trotters in France. My venture into Spain wasn't quite so successful, as the tradition there is not to pay for your horse until it has won a race. We didn't stop at horses though – my good pal Noel Pearson staged *Joseph and the Amazing Technicolor Dreamcoat* in

Goffs. It ran for three months, complete with camels and sand, and we had concerts also, including Don McLean.

And it worked. It all worked. The effect on the market of Goffs' new way of doing things was instantaneous. There were some who complained the new structure was too modern, who didn't like the emphasis on entertaining and the way we deliberately targeted the international, high end of the market, but there was no disputing the evidence. Prices rocketed almost immediately, across the board, and in 1984 we sold a yearling for a record 3.1 million guineas. That was Authaal, a son of Shergar, and the best of his progeny, who went on to win the Irish St Leger in 1986. He had been sold the previous winter at Goffs as a foal, for 325,000 guineas, and was then bought as a yearling by Sheikh Mohammed for the record amount, with Vincent O'Brien as the under-bidder. Another year, Stavros Niarchos, the Greek billionaire, bought a half-sister to Shirley Heights, the Derby winner, from us.

Shergar himself played a small but memorable role in my life too, after he was kidnapped. Like a number of prominent people in the bloodstock industry, I was asked by the IBBA to liaise with police around the possibility of his return, which entailed some months of being contacted by clairvoyants, chancers and gangsters from across the world. Shergar, more than almost any other horse I have come across, had captured the public imagination after winning the Epsom Derby in 1981 by a spectacular ten lengths. He was named European Horse of the Year the same year and put to stud at the Ballymany Stud in the Curragh. On the night of 8 February 1983, masked gunmen, probably IRA, drove a horsebox into the yard at Ballymany and rang the doorbell of Shergar's groom, James Fitzgerald. They held his family at gunpoint while forcing Fitzgerald to help them load Shergar into the horsebox, which was then driven off. Fitzgerald was put into a car and driven around for three hours, terrorised by the gunmen, before being thrown out onto the road some seven miles from the stud with the password the men said they would use in negotiations.

Why the horse was not better protected, I will never know. After he was paraded through the streets following his Newmarket win, the whole country knew about him and how valuable he was, yet he was kept somewhere that it became clear afterwards had inadequate security.

Anyway, in the general bungling and mismanagement that followed, it seemed that everyone from Alan Dukes, the local TD and Minister for Finance, and Michael Noonan, Minister for Justice, were rung, but not the gardaí. Not for eight hours. By that time, the trail, such as it was, had gone cold and was very hard to read. The day chosen by the kidnappers – cleverly – was also the day of the only horse sale in the spring in the country, which meant there were horseboxes on nearly every highway and byway in the country, and also crossing over the border.

The thieves wanted £5 million for Shergar's safe return, but they hadn't realised that he was owned by a syndicate rather than outright by the Aga Khan, as they had thought. A reward of £250,000 was offered for information leading to his recovery – I'd say a fairly mythical £250,000, because the members of the syndicate were very clear from the start that they were not

My grandparents, Wing Commander Tim Stanley-Clarke and
Marnie, on their wedding day – note the bride's black cloak.

Pippa Stanley-Clarke, my mother.

Me with my dad.

Me aged sixteen.

My wedding day with Mikaela, Cheyne Walk, London.

Luke (standing) and Pirate in Ivy House, Leixlip.

Me with Lester Piggott and Vincent O'Brien at Phoenix Park Racecourse.

Me and Mary-Ann with Lily at Landscape House, Kilsheelan, home of Mary-Ann's parents, Phonsie and Ann O'Brien.

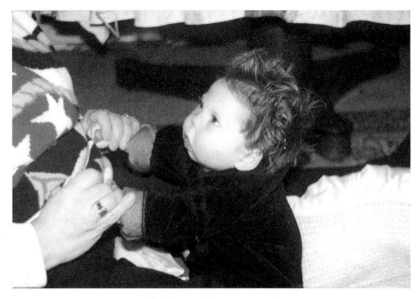

Jack at eighteen months.

Sam in Paris.

Molly on Riverview Annie, Fontainbleu 2013.

Me with Mary-Ann and Bill Clinton,
on one of his many visits to Dublin.

Me receiving the Charity of the Year Award 2003.

going to pay any ransom, on the basis that no racehorse in the country would be safe if they did. However, it was enough to flush out all sorts of peculiar people, from as far away as Tunisia and Australia, all claiming to have information.

Captain Seán Berry, a retired army captain who was the manager of the Bloodstock Breeders, took on the role of negotiator, although he wasn't the only one. In the general mayhem and free-for-all that followed Shergar's kidnapping, there were at least three negotiators, including a couple of racing journalists. At one stage Shergar's vet, Stan Cosgrove, was dispatched to collect evidence that the horse was still alive from a hotel reception, only for the gang to be scared off by a very obvious Special Branch presence.

All the same, Seán Berry spent several months being inundated with calls from people claiming to be in the IRA, to know people who were, or to have psychic powers or special information. He even had two clairvoyants travel over from San Francisco and stay with him for a few days, as they tried to persuade their spirit guides to divulge something useful. He received threats, veiled hints and innuendos, and the police insisted he record every phone call, which wasn't at all easy in those days. At one point he was sent to a kiosk in Monasterevin to take a call from the gang, who said they would meet him in Portumna in Galway. They told him to bring the £250,000, but he refused, saying that he needed to see that Shergar was still alive and that, if a horse was produced, it was indeed Shergar and not some substitute. That came to nothing as well, and eventually the nine-day wonder began to die down.

It seems clear now that Shergar was dead within a few days of being taken. He was a nervous, highly strung thoroughbred stallion, a very different prospect to a farm horse or average riding horse, and probably terrifying to any one not used to such animals. The most likely story is that he went demented in his horsebox, injured a leg, and was shot on the spot. A pitiful end for such a magnificent animal. However, gone but not forgotten; as recently as December 2013, approaching the thirty-first anniversary of the kidnap, I was interviewed by Marian Finucane. Such is the hold he still has on the public imagination.

Another memorable moment came in 1982, when the IRA planted two bombs in Hyde Park and Regent's Park. The bombs exploded during military ceremonies, killing four soldiers of the Blues & Royals and seven bandsmen of the Royal Green Jackets. Seven of the Blues & Royals' horses also died. That was one of the many very low moments in Irish–British relations, and at the time I thought it important that England should realise that many Irish people felt real horror at this incident.

I talked to Paddy McGrath, Goffs' chairman, and suggested that we open a private fund to replace the seven horses that had been killed. We couldn't, alas, replace the men, but we thought that this would be a gesture of sorts. Paddy and the board were in agreement, so I wrote to Colonel Andrew Parker Bowles, then commanding officer of the Blues & Royals, who I knew a bit, and asked if this idea would be acceptable. He said it would – in fact he called the offer 'genuine and heart-warming' – and so we established a fund through the RDS and raised £47,000 from private donations. The cheque went from the RDS to the British Embassy and bought six cavalry horses from Wexford. Horses have always been a kind of common ground between Ireland and England, and I thought this would be a quiet, but symbolic, way of joining hands across the sea.

When the announcement was made at the Dublin Horse Show that year, there were loud cheers from the crowd, which showed me that I was right in believing that many Irish people were appalled by what had happened.

Another big deal for the new Goffs was the dispersal sale of Alan Clore, industrialist and only son of Sir Charles Clore. He was one of the big losers from Black Monday in 1987, when his ambitious scheme to gain control of KaiserTech resulted in financial disaster. Among his other businesses and investments, Clore had around 300 horses in France, Ireland and the US, comprising mares, foals and stallions. The bank needed to sell his horses quickly and gave the job to Fasig-Tipton and Goffs. So my old friend John Finney and I came up with a scheme to sell the horses almost simultaneously, by telecast, rather than going to the expense of shipping them all to the one sales yard. We sold the whole catalogue via the sales rings of Deauville, Goffs and Kentucky as though the horses were in the one spot. That was 1987, and we had people sitting in Goffs, bidding on a mare being paraded around the ring in Deauville, or a colt in Kentucky. We had to put up a big satellite dish in the grounds of Goffs, just outside my window. An engineer from California came to oversee the whole thing, and at one point I looked out of the window to see our groundsman, Mickey Bugles, taking a sledgehammer to the base of the dish, trying to get it to fit, while the engineer looked on in horror.

During those years, we closed the gap between ourselves and Tattersalls, very much the market leaders. Where they might have been turning over around £80 million annually, we began to hover at around £60 million, something that was extraordinary, given the long history Goffs had of being the poor relation. Later, the gap widened again considerably, and to put that into context, in recent years Tattersalls would have done around £140 million, while Goffs was down around £40 million, as it reverted to the slightly sleepy place it originally was, and Tattersalls, always the market leader, gained ground again.

Despite the few who carped, who disliked the money being spent entertaining high-profile international buyers and the emphasis on the invitation-only sales, we had been very careful to keep the smaller breeder in mind too. After all, the whole point of entertaining these buyers was so they would come and buy our horses. What we did with the yearling market was really to educate people. The big guys knew all about the marketing of their horses, how to prepare them, lead them out, these basic things that go on at the sales that make all the difference to the final price. The small breeders – guys who had two or three mares – didn't know this stuff, probably didn't have a brand name and had never bothered with it before, but we professionalised the whole area of selling horses and encouraged everyone to show their horses better, prepare them better, groom them better, even get them in on time. It was surprising just how many breeders didn't think that was important. We also insisted that the sales paddocks were better dressed, with the stud farms producing professional signs rather than something hand-written on cardboard. To the bigger breeders we dedicated entertainment suites at the end of each barn.

Despite the startling success of the new Goffs, in the early 1980s the bloodstock market worldwide started to flag. At Goffs the aggregate from the sales dropped appallingly and the company began to lose money. I realised that the game needed another level of excitement; it was all getting a bit flabby and needed a vehicle to spark up interest again. Around that time, I read about a company, based in Queensland, Australia, that had invented something they called the Magic Million. This was a sale of local pedigree horses, of no international interest, but it had been given a great kick by the fact that these horses were then the only ones eligible to run in a race with million-dollar prize money the following year. In there was the kernel of a truly brilliant idea, but I knew we would have to bring it upmarket, treat it as a production and style it up into an irresistible business idea.

We managed to get Cartier on board, having tried and failed to attract a number of other sponsor brands, and largely thanks to Anthony Marangos, the Greek boy who had been at Stonehouse with me and was now managing director. They didn't put in any actual money, but they paid for all the publicity including the fabulous cocktail parties in Claridges, Beverley Hills and Paris to promote the event. And their name was exactly the guarantee of quality and glamour that we needed, a stamp of approval that would resonate with the new rich around the world – the very people we needed to attract. The Cartier Million had a ring to it that Goffs Million simply didn't.

The concept was a very simple one – find 250 yearlings of sufficient quality to be sold at a special yearling sale in Goffs. Out of those only twenty would be eligible the following year to race as two-year-olds, for total prize money of £1 million. They would qualify by having shown themselves to be the top twenty performers of their year. Doing it that way meant that the large owner-breeders, for example, couldn't suddenly swoop in with some brilliant horse bred by themselves and scoop up the money. Suddenly, bloodstock agents and trainers had a story that was easy to explain to their owners. These 250 horses, even if they were as slow as old men, were the only ones eligible to run, and as we paid out down to tenth place, the odds were clearly pretty attractive. So attractive that this really was the birth of syndicates as we know them now. Until then, a few very rich people had sometimes got together to buy a particular horse, but from then on it became something that dentists, taxi drivers, ordinary people did. It's fair to say we created a whole new market, giving new blood, new life and new excitement to the industry. At the time, I was managing Phoenix Park Racecourse as well as my job with Goffs, because Vincent O'Brien had asked me to step in when his manager had to leave suddenly due to family illness, and that was the perfect spot for the race: close to the city centre, an elegant site, the one glamour track we had.

Cartier would handle the marketing, but Goffs were responsible for the actual money – to be raised from entry fees to the sale, entry fees to the race and higher sales commission. This, against the backdrop that the company was losing money, meant it wasn't an easy sell internally at all. Also, we had to find 250 horses of sufficient quality: not easy either. Drastic measures were called for. First, I vowed to give up drink – except for champagne – until we had our horses, and then I sent agents far and wide, including to Scandinavia and the UK, to entice any decent bloodstock. In general though, we managed to hide how desperate we were for horses and, somehow, we did it; the first sale really took off, was a runaway success and helped all segments of the market. And I went back on the drink. True to form, the Establishment did everything to stop the project, led by the Senior Steward of the British Jockey Club, Lord Fairhaven, who attacked the concept, and me, at a smart horse dinner in Paris, all because it would be worth double the Epsom Derby. Luckily, the last roar of the mangy lion.

I think that project took me through the entire rainbow of emotions. It was such a novel idea that people thought I was a lunatic at first – only one person supported me from the start, the trainer Tommy Stack. Every time I doubted myself, it seemed as if by magic he would ring that very day and say, 'Don't you dare lose it; this is the answer.' I had to use unbelievable diplomacy and patience to persuade my financial controller to have faith in me and my ability to deliver, because the project could have bankrupted Goffs. I became enormously excited once we saw the calibre of horse being entered in the sale and the calibre of vendor we were attracting. I was grateful to the trainers and bloodstock agents who went out and sang the song, and I'm indebted to the racing journalists who really understood the potential and made certain that the spotlight was on the Cartier Million race for months ahead. The day after the first day of the Cartier sale, by which time I knew that we had a wild success on our hands, I was so tired that I found myself in floods of tears in my bath that morning. A combination of relief and exhaustion just wiped me out.

We shamelessly hyped the Million sale. It was held over three days, sandwiched between Newmarket and the Arc de Triomphe, two major events in the horsy calendar, so we laid on a private plane, a 737, to get people from one to the other via us – a very big gig in those days. During the day, we had the Premier level and then the Sportsman level, with the Million in the evenings. But of course once the really rich guys were there for the Million, they naturally cast their eye over the other horses on offer and if they happened to spot a nice yearling in the Premier sale, well, they were very likely to snap it up. Turnover for Goffs went from around £23 million to £45 million, and everyone was happy.

The following year, it was apparent that people's loyalty evaporated completely once the cheque from Goffs was bigger than the cheque from Tattersalls. We got a whole new rush of breeders trying to get into the next year's Cartier, guys who had previously only ever sold with Tattersalls. We were really on the way. And Cartier more than lived up to their end of the bargain. The marketing and entertaining they did around the Million was so good that we had all sorts of fascinating people turn up: I remember Joan Collins coming along with 'Bungalow' Bill Wiggins; Helmut Newton and his Amazonian wife, June; Ringo Starr one year; Pandora and Charles Delevingne, parents of Poppy and Cara; Richard Harris; and actor Peter Bowles, who played Richard in *To the Manor Born* and the lead in *The Irish R.M.* There was always a lunch in Luttrellstown and more helicopters than you could shake a stick at, because after the lunch everyone flew down to the Phoenix Park. We were way ahead of the times in terms of the emphasis on glamour and beauty.

Tattersalls copied us after the second year, with their own version, with Tiffany as their sponsor, but in those days they were ill at ease with marketing and didn't seem to understand that it was not just a matter of staging one race on one particular day of the year. However, even though they didn't do it very well – not nearly as well as us – that cheapened things rather. But much worse was in store. Paddy McGrath had always been chairman of the board while I was at Goffs, and he and I got on very well together. Once I was able to convince him to do a particular thing, he would then stand by me throughout. But a lot of things were going wrong in the McGrath lives at that time, including Waterford Glass, the Sweepstakes and Avair. Paddy decided to step down from the board, despite my efforts to convince him to stay. His replacement was Michael Dargan, a lifetime civil servant, with whom I simply had nothing in common.

Where we really fell down, Dargan and I, was over the

Cartier Million. He believed it was quite wrong that Cartier wasn't putting any actual cash into the deal, whereas I knew that the value to Goffs of their name and marketing was enough. Dargan commissioned a consultant to put a value on the association and when the contract came up for renewal he tried to charge Cartier money to stay involved. Naturally, and as I knew they would, they politely declined, and so the Cartier Million was no more. It only lasted three years – Dermot Weld won it twice, Tommy Stack once – and when it was gone I didn't see much point in staying on myself. Dargan and I were never going to get along and I was very disappointed that such a wonderful and successful idea should have been killed off through what I thought was unnecessary greed. I was also very disappointed with the board, who didn't support me. That really showed me the weakness of any CEO who doesn't have a very large shareholding in the company – you are at the mercy of people who don't understand what you're trying to do. Seán Collins, renowned vet and studmaster, flew back from his holidays to try to persuade the board that they were crazy, but they wouldn't listen. That was the end of the Cartier Million, and a big mistake it was too. The proof was in the pudding – the following year the turnover of the company fell by 41 per cent.

I was genuinely upset. Although I had never had any money invested there, I had created Goffs, put the syndicate together and run it as one of the top sales companies in the world. I felt that it was my baby, regardless of the shareholders, and that it wouldn't have been there at all if it wasn't for me and my persuasive powers. The Cartier Million was another baby, and I couldn't believe that someone who had nothing to do with any of it could come along and make decisions about its future and not listen to me. It took Goffs six months to find a new managing director, who then also left after a year or two.

Sad as I was, I was also slightly bored by Goffs after so many years, and after the success of the Million there was unlikely to be another challenging mountain. I had been sort of thinking about going, but I wish it hadn't happened that way. Sadly Phoenix Park Racecourse closed the year after, and so, after thirty-five wonderful years, my life in the horse world came to an end. I had a magnificent run, and I dearly hoped that the second leg of the relay race, the young men and women coming up behind me, would pick up the baton and go even faster. Sadly that didn't really happen. Goffs had many rather slow years after that, and racing in general badly needs a shot in the arm at the moment. The age profile is too old and, so far, efforts made to attract a younger, dynamic crowd haven't really been successful. But for me, the time had clearly come to move on.

9

Ryanair and
the Sports Council

The first time I met Tony Ryan was at a dinner party given by Mary Scott, who had been married to Niall Scott, the architect who built Goffs, and was now living near Kilternan. We were asked to dinner to meet someone described as the new, young, up-and-coming star of the Irish commercial world. That was Tony Ryan, who was tired and emotional that night, and ended up falling asleep in his pea soup. But I came to know him better after that, and found that he was one of the most extraordinary people I have met. To me, the Renaissance man. He was very interesting, passionate and engaged, with a great eye for paintings – we favoured a few of the same young, emerging Irish artists – and furniture, and he had a very obvious flair for business. At the time he was with Miranda Guinness, who I had known since I was young and always thought was a really special, wonderful person.

Tony invited me out to lunch in Greene's, off Jermyn Street in London, shortly after I left Goffs and persuaded me to join the airline that he pretended wasn't his, although his name seemed to be on the fuselage (this was for tax reasons; there was no doubt really as to whom the airline belonged, certainly not in the minds of anyone who worked for it) – Ryanair. I was to be the marketing director, with the object of making it one of the smartest small airlines in Europe.

Yes, the idea seems a hilarious one now, but truly, that was the plan at the time. Tony wanted Ryanair to become synonymous with luxury, quality and impeccable customer service. It sounded like a good idea to me and I agreed to come on board. I didn't know anything about flying, except that I'd flown as much as anyone in the world by then.

When I started in the job, it was quite obvious that Ryanair was losing a lot of money. The CEO then was P. J. McGoldrick, a charming man and a great pilot, and the financial controller was Michael O'Leary. Now, I wasn't really a professional – I was just a blow-in – but I could tell pretty quickly that they were very uncertain how they were going to stop this airline simply bleeding to death. Tony's plan – to go upmarket – was one possibility, but I began quite soon to see that it didn't find favour with everyone. Michael O'Leary was already convinced of what would be his great stroke of genius – to go for something we'd never heard of at that time in Europe then – no-frills flying. Cheap, cheap, cheap air travel, such as was done internally in the States by Southwest Airlines. It was a clever, original idea, one that worked – as we all know – very well.

So, right from the start, I was very much a happy square peg in a round hole. I lived in a sort of cupboard for the first three months, with a computer called Yield Control, and no secretary or PA. I didn't really understand the in-house airline language – in which I wasn't 'Jonathan Irwin', I had some other designation I can't remember – and I used to get all sorts of memorandums, which I merrily threw in the bin, because they clearly weren't for me. I lived happily with Yield Control for a while, and then after about four months I got a secretary who actually knew something about the business, which definitely helped. I also noticed that I was very high up on the telephone lists which were printed and circulated every week. I thought this was a good thing, but actually it was a very bad thing – it meant I was spending more money on the phone than anyone else. I tried explaining that as marketing director, my job was to be on the phone, but they weren't buying that.

Like everyone else who worked for Tony Ryan, I was summoned to dramatic weekly meetings with him down at Kilboy, in Tipperary. These weren't as bad as the regular Monday morning meetings he conducted during the Guinness Peat Aviation (GPA) days – more blood-lettings than get-togethers, still remembered with a shudder, I'd say, by those ordered in to them – but they were intense all the same. The meetings seemed to me just an exercise in humiliating his senior management. Once, he was distraught because we were flying ATRs (very expensive Italian prop planes) and he was ashamed to be associated with, as he put it, a taxi company, and he insisted that we must immediately hire in Romanian BAC 1-11s. And so this would be done. The changeover in the fleet of ATRs to 1-11s was a nightmarish and lengthy process, and by the time the BAC 1-11s were about to come on stream, he would have hysterics about a taxi service being extravagant enough to fly jet planes. Chaos, frankly! However, for all his table-thumping, or maybe because of it, Tony Ryan definitely inspired hero worship in other men. Some of the more ambitious young employees would even dress like him, in double-breasted suits with top-pocket silk handkerchiefs. They put on the same mannerisms and types of behaviour, even pretending to an interest in culture, art and the restoration of old houses.

I was living on Burlington Road at that stage and, having always been an early riser, I used to walk over and generally be in the office on Nassau Street at about 6 a.m. Michael O'Leary would always be there ahead of me. Except for one day, when I arrived at about 5.30 a.m. and he wasn't there. The next day, I arrived at 5.30 a.m. again, and there he was. He clearly wasn't going to be beaten on virtue by me. We seemed to get into this extraordinary sort of early-rising match, and I was convinced that it would all spiral out of control, that one day I would come in at 2.30 a.m., then he would come in at 2 a.m., and soon we would be coming back into work almost before we left the night before. He also ran everywhere in his stockinged feet. The office was L-shaped, with reception at the apex of the L. Michael would charge off without any shoes, past reception and into the coupon department.

I had some bright and brilliant ideas while I was at Ryanair, the best of which, I think, was, instead of having the usual mainly white fuselage, to envelope the entire fuselage in royal blue, which is actually a traditional Irish colour, with a golden harp on the tail fin. We would have had, visually, the smartest public aircraft seen anywhere, even smarter than Royal Jordanian, and while people might not have known who we were to start with, we would have fast become a kind of upmarket Eddie Stobart of the air. It would have been a real marketing coup, but sadly no one else bought into the entire idea. They did paint the tail fin blue, with a golden harp, but that was as far as they would go.

Another of my great ideas, which I brought up at one of the weekly meetings in Kilboy, was based around my knowledge of how much the English love their dogs. At that time, they couldn't take their dogs anywhere on holiday with them, except for Ireland, because of the quarantine laws. I felt this was something we could really exploit and make work for us, so my plan was, why don't we have a dog service? Fly the dogs over for free in the hold, and in doing so make ourselves a more attractive destination for English people who hate to be parted from their four-legged friends. Genius. Until Michael knocked it on the head, quite rightly, by explaining that in the planes we were flying – BAC1-11s – the hold isn't pressurised, so the dogs wouldn't survive the trip and their owners, instead of being grateful, would find themselves confronted by a whole load of four-legged cadavers and be furious.

Shortly after that, I began to get the feeling that Ireland was about to become a great golf centre, which indeed it has become, so I suggested we become a golfing airline, specially catering for such holidays, but Michael shot that down on the basis that the handling and space required for unwieldy things like golf bags made it impossible to make any money.

My last brilliant idea was to let old age pensioners basically fly for nothing, because the airline needed a soft side and pensioners travel free on buses, so why not let them travel free on our planes, but Michael was against that too.

That was really the end of it for me. I lasted about a year and really enjoyed it – it was a totally different world, but it wasn't for me. And they knew it wasn't for me. I think that was very obvious quite early on, but they treated me very well and I had a good deal of fun.

After that, despite being the most unathletic person in the world, and having sworn a solemn oath that I would never again do a day's exercise once I left Eton, I found myself as head of something called the Dublin Sports Council.

Tony O'Reilly and Gay Mitchell approached me; Gay was lord mayor of Dublin at the time, and the two of them had come up with the idea of setting up a sports council, with the objective of attracting major sporting events into Dublin and examining the possibility of Ireland one day making a bid to hold the Olympics: basically, trying to create 'good news' in 1993. I think it was Gay's idea originally, and he managed to sell O'Reilly on it. Both felt it was a disgrace that Ireland, particularly Dublin, should have so few decent sporting venues.

It was an excellent idea – but a tall order. The year was 1993 and the country had very few decent sporting facilities. We had Croke Park and Lansdowne Road, but neither had been done up and, compared to other venues of their type around Europe, they were way out of date. There was no Olympic-sized swimming pool, no ice rink, no basketball arena and no top-class athletics track. Our job was, despite the many drawbacks, to showcase Ireland as the kind of place where really big sporting fixtures – major league games – could be played and would find the kind of support and standards they were used to.

Working with me was Kieran McLoughlin, one of the most gifted and amusing of people, who I seconded from the Dublin Chamber of Commerce and who was later headhunted by O'Reilly to become CEO of the Ireland Funds worldwide, where he still is. Neither Kieran nor I could run faster than the fat man – we must have been the two most unfit men in Ireland – but we set off on this mission, designed a logo and got to work.

We were given offices in Clare Street by the Dublin Chamber of Commerce, and attracted a large tranche of private money from an American namesake of mine, James B. Irwin. He was chairman of Integrated Control Systems Inc., known as IMPAC, and founder of the IMPAC Literary Award, and very sadly killed himself in 2009, some time after his son was tragically murdered. I remember one very odd boat trip with him and a host of American generals as we sailed down to see a Westpoint football game. Jim spent most of the journey up and down locked in the saloon with the four-star generals, neglecting his other guests. God knows what they were discussing.

Kieran and I ran this organisation for three years. We had the best of fun and a lot of successes. We attracted the 1994 Ladies' World Hockey Games and the 1998 Tour de France, thanks to Pat McQuaid, who became president of the World

Cycling Federation and was very good to work with. That was huge, with people lining the roads for miles to see these remarkable athletes (if rather more assisted than we knew then). We brought darts to Ireland, a fairly niche game at the time, but one that attracts huge numbers now. Sadly it was sneered at by the National Sports Council as 'not the sort of sport we want in Ireland'.

Gay Mitchell had always wanted Ireland to make a bid for the Olympics, and so I got ninety of Ireland's finest to agree to sit on various committees – a finance committee, a transport committee and so on, to look into the feasibility of such a thing. These were the early 1990s, and the bid was to be for 2016. The committees made their reports – not enough roads, not enough hotels, not enough venues, all of which was true, but they also laid down a very good blueprint for what the city needed, much of which has now been delivered, almost to the exact time frame the report identified. Every single committee thought that we wouldn't disgrace ourselves by making a bid. I still think those ninety people saw the future. I'm not saying we could host the Olympics, but we could certainly bid for it and not expect to be laughed out of court. Apart from the infrastructure, which has improved hugely, we had some serious points in our favour – the time zones were great, we have no imperial history of being horrible to other countries and we are non-aligned in international political terms. Exactly the same things that worked so well for us during so many Eurovision song contests, until the whole thing became just too silly, would have worked for an Olympic bid too. The president of the International Olympic Committee (IOC), Pat Hickey, dismissed our ideas. In the end, he was probably right – although I believe our bid was a credible one, and I think it would have been a good idea for Ireland to bid if only in order to encourage the improvement in sporting infrastructure. Pat has become a good friend since, and to my mind is perhaps the smartest and most astute sports administrator in Ireland, recognised by his rapid rise through the ranks of the IOC.

Later I did have some experience of a successful Olympic bid when Denis O'Brien asked would I become chairman of the Venues Committee of the Special Olympic World Games, because by then I probably knew more about the matter than anyone else.

One of our biggest gigs was bringing the first major American college football game here, Notre Dame v US Navy in 1996. Michael Smurfit, Tom Kane, who owned Adare Manor, and one or two others, put up £3 million for that. Notre Dame were amazed by Croke Park. Only one stand was built then, but they had played all over America and had seen nothing like it. They couldn't get over the splendour of the locker rooms and the avenue built underneath specifically for ambulances so as to ensure speedy medical access. We attracted the largest ever invasion of North Americans for that game – some 22,000. Eleven thousand had to stay in Dublin, and 11,000 in the country, and then we swapped them around midway through their stay, so everyone got to experience both sides of the country.

The week before the game, disaster struck when somebody

rang me to ask had I not realised that US college football games were 'dry': alcohol was usually a complete no-no. Well, the possibility of getting any Irishman to come and see a game he hardly knows, which lasts four hours, with no booze – it really didn't bear thinking about. NBC were already giving us hell because they didn't want the stands to be empty, and of course the teams would have kicked up a terrific fuss. Somehow, we got over that hurdle and got a licence, but I lost about two stone in two days, and even now I don't quite know how we did it and don't really want to ask. In the end, we all had a great time. Twenty-two thousand Americans sat outside in the pouring rain watching the game, while the Irish sat inside in the bar having a wonderful time. There was a mass of diddley-aye music, and a great atmosphere. The game itself didn't make money, but was a huge success and showed what could be done.

And then there was the one that got away. This is the one that means the most to me – because it was an utterly brilliant idea that never came off, and because it was the brainwave of my son, Sam Fortune. Then aged nine, he showed himself throughout his too-short life to be of exceptional ability. It was a bid to lure Wimbledon FC, then owned by a Lebanese family, the Hammams, without a home ground or many fans, but playing in the Premier Division, to relocate to Dublin. And really, we got within a whisker of getting them here. The Hammams themselves were very keen. Once Sam explained the idea to me – and he had worked out the entire strategy – I got a syndicate together that was going to build a stadium for 40,000 seats in Clondalkin, and donate €15 million to the

Football Association of Ireland (FAI) for junior and schoolboy soccer. I also did a deal with my old friends Ryanair that they would offer free transport to Dublin for two seasons to the few registered supporters of Wimbledon FC. We were going to rename the team the Dublin Dons, and they would have been playing Arsenal, Man Utd, Everton, so that even if no Irish person was willing to come along and watch the Dons in the early days, they would have packed the stadium to see the teams the Dons were playing against. We would have had household-name footballers here every fortnight. It was really a wonderful idea. Quickly, we would have had the tills going ching-ching, and have had funds to upgrade the players. Indeed Lansdowne Marketing found 72 per cent of people in favour of it, and the Dublin Chamber of Commerce thought it worth £22 million a year to the city. But the FAI wouldn't even meet us – they said it would ruin local Irish soccer – and so it came to nothing. Dublin remains a soccer-mad city with no international team. Tragic.

Soon after, an international stadium (the Bertie Bowl), a potentially great sports campus that I was very supportive of, came to nothing, and we found, more and more, that trying to raise money was really very difficult, even though Kieran and I were both pretty good at it. Because the Sports Council was closely associated with Tony O'Reilly, there was a very definite attitude of, 'Well, if O'Reilly wants to do it, let him do it himself ...' But O'Reilly had given as much money as he was going to, as had James Irwin, and finally it all began to run out of steam and had to be mothballed.

10

MARY-ANN

The first time I met Mary-Ann O'Brien was thoroughly inauspicious, and memorable only for the wrong reasons. She was at that time in her early twenties, very bohemian and, as she says herself, rather off the wall. Certainly she was a daughter to cause disquiet to her clever, hard-working parents, Phonsie and Ann. They have spent their entire lives successfully training National Hunt horses, and were worried that she lacked direction and focus in life. In an effort to set her on the right path, Phonsie managed to persuade me to meet her, in my capacity as CEO of Goffs, to see if there was any kind of role there for her. She was refusing to settle down or pick any kind of career for herself, and they thought a steady job in a firm like Goffs would help her make up her mind before she became terminally unemployable.

As Mary-Ann remembers it, she was forced into a 'dreadful' tweed skirt with a pale blue shirt which she hated, and in she came to meet me. As far as she was concerned, here was this man who looked like a boiled egg in a stuffed shirt, with a pompous accent, and she couldn't wait to get out. I, meanwhile, thought she was a hideous, appalling communist, and I couldn't wait to get her out of my office. We got through the interview, somehow, then both ran in opposite directions.

Mary-Ann went off around the world about four times, and had about fifty different jobs, and the next time we met was years later, when I was managing the Phoenix Park Racecourse as a kind of emergency CEO, at the request of Vincent O'Brien. Mary-Ann was Vincent's niece, and back in Ireland by then. She started as receptionist, then became marketing manager. By the time I met her again, she had become incredibly hard-working and entrepreneurial, applying all her undoubted brilliance to making the Phoenix Park Racecourse a financial success, which I think is where we really started to connect. I remember she was superb at getting sponsorship for every single race run at the Park, and we worked together on a big rock concert, with the Eurythmics and U2, then still relatively unknown. We found that we got on fantastically well, and I remember once saying to her, 'I know your older sister Gillian, and then there is Yvonne, but what happened to that appalling communist who came in to my office that time?'

'Jonathan, that was me.'

That was around 1984, and that's how it all started. It must sound too pathetic for words – a middle-aged man in his mackintosh, and the secretary. Except that of course since then Mary-Ann has created a worldwide brand and become a senator, so now I have to walk two steps behind her.

Certainly, she played no part in my divorce (Mikaela and I were already separated by then and Mikaela had moved to London long before that), except insomuch as I was, during the end of my marriage to Mikaela, enormously lonely, because the companion of my life had slightly removed herself. At home, I seemed to be the worst in the world, whereas at work there was this other girl who seemed to think I was still quite amusing, not just a soapsud that's gone down the drain. It's important to feel that somebody finds you interesting and amusing; life is just too depressing otherwise.

I always say that Mary-Ann and I have nothing in common whatsoever, and yet we never fight. We're both non-confrontational and we understand that even if you 'win' the fight, you're probably going to be exhausted and need a lie-down. Even though we have been through some very hard things together, I don't think we've ever had a row. I got quite cross recently when she spent €700 buying a Chihuahua, because I hate Chihuahuas, and there was a lot of stamping feet and getting out of cars in a huff then, but now I'm actually quite fond of him. Other than that, although I say we have nothing in common, actually, I think we see the world in a similar way – we rate the same kinds of things as important and the same kinds of things as trivial.

Once our daughter Lily was born, we got an apartment in the stable yard at Carton House. At the time it was rather rundown, and owned by Lee Mallaghan – a very nice man who later became a trustee of the Jack and Jill Foundation; I think Mary-Ann had done some catering for him, which is where she heard about the property. Lee had tried to get planning permission for a whole variety of projects but nothing had come through for him yet. There we were, in this beautiful apartment in 1,100 acres, and with Marianne Faithfull as our only neighbour at Shell Cottage by the lake, perhaps one of the most haunted houses I've ever visited in my life. The setting was idyllic, but all was not as wonderful as you'd expect.

Lily was a little baby and Mary-Ann had developed a bad case of ME after the birth. The girl I first met, who could work seven days a week and still go out all night, with energy and dynamism to burn, constantly bursting with ideas and enthusiasm, became so exhausted that getting down the spiral staircase of our apartment once a day was the most she could do. She didn't have enough mental energy to read the newspaper – and I'm not talking *The Irish Times* here, even the *Star* was too much for her. She barely went outside the house for two years.

I know ME still gets a lot of bad press as some kind of psychosomatic ailment, a fantasy illness for hysterical women – and back then, that attitude was much, much worse and Mary-Ann could hardly get a single doctor to take her seriously – but in fact ME is a very real, very debilitating condition. She doesn't really remember the first two-and-a-half years of Lily's life; she was constantly exhausted and in almost constant pain. The one good thing was that her sister Gillian, a racehorse trainer, had the same thing at the same time, and so they were able to buck each other up and keep each other going. That really saved their bacon: they were able to rely on each other because everyone else said, 'That doesn't exist, pull yourselves together!' And these are two of the most practical, hard-working, dynamic women ever. That is certainly the most damaging thing you can do –

tell someone their dreadful plight is 'just' psychosomatic, when actually it's like a dreadful black tunnel you can't get out of.

They both went to see Dr Paschal Carmody, rather a controversial doctor, who was later taken to court on charges of obtaining money through falsely pretending that he could cure cancer. He was cleared of all the charges after a legal battle that lasted nine years. Anyway, Mary-Ann and Gillian both went to him, and he made a big difference to their health, partly because he took their symptoms seriously and partly because he filled them up with strange herbs, and they came through. Mary-Ann still has to be very careful about stress, because your immune system will never fully recover from something like that; it lingers on. But the very roughest time came to an end, and when, towards the end of Lily's third year, Mary-Ann seemed to be getting better, I thought a holiday in South Africa would be nice.

We ended up staying in a beautiful family-run hotel in Hermanus, the very same place that my mother, Pippa, first went to when her family moved to South Africa for their strange sort of gap year when she was a child. A Rhodesian family owned the hotel, and the eldest daughter and Mary-Ann became great pals. One day Mary-Ann saw a beautiful chess set at the reception, and asked could she take it out to the pool to play a game with me. The daughter laughed and said, 'Well you could, but it's made out of chocolate and will melt ...' Then Mary-Ann discovered that the daughter was a master chocolatier, which really caught her imagination, so she spent the next four or five days in the kitchen, in her bikini, learning how to do the simple things with chocolate, how to melt it, temper it and so on. We bought a few moulds in Cape Town, and when we came back here, Mary-Ann made chocolates for Easter and sold them at fairs around the countryside, where they seemed to be very popular.

From there she started making chocolates regularly at Carton, and one day plucked up enough courage to go down to Superquinn in Lucan and see the manager John Foy. He said, rather doubtfully I suspect, 'Well, we'll give you a chance, but you know, all our chocolates are Belgian ...' Within about a year, all their chocolates were Lily O'Brien's.

Superquinn were very good clients and things started getting quite serious. Clearly, the kitchen of the apartment in Carton Demesne wasn't going to work any more. As it happened, before the Phoenix Park Racecourse closed in 1990, they had put in brand new, very good kitchens. So Mary-Ann asked Vincent O'Brien, her uncle, if she could use them. She also found two lovely old ladies who had worked with Urney's, a chocolate company that had been based in Tallaght, before being bought out by Unilever and closed down in 1980, and started her chocolate business rather more seriously.

Around that same time, the first of the terrible tragedies that were to come into our lives, hit. Mary-Ann was heavily pregnant with twins and she knew something was wrong. She asked the hospital to take her in for nearly a full week before they finally agreed to do so. They scanned her that morning and could only find one heartbeat. One of the twins was dead. Even so, they didn't perform a caesarean section until that evening, leaving Mary-Ann and me to spend an entire day devastated by the news and distraught at the very real possibility that the other twin wouldn't survive either. With twin-to-twin transfusion, this was a very real possibility. Finally the caesarean was carried out. John was stillborn on 1 February 1994 and Phonsie was taken to intensive care for two weeks.

I was so ignorant in those days, had led a life so mercifully free from heartbreak, that I didn't even know stillborn children were buried. I will never forget the misery of getting through that funeral, of carrying his little white coffin under my arm, and burying this poor baby who never lived at all.

We buried him in the tiny graveyard at Ballinure, about ten minutes from where we live, and one of the prettiest graveyards in Ireland. It looks down into a beautiful valley. Later, after Jack died, we put a garden bench in there, dedicated to our two boys, John and Jack. I hoped that people might, on a beautiful day, sit there for a while and gaze down into the valley. When I drive by and see people doing just that, it makes me feel happy.

We were desperately sad, but fortunate to have one wonderful child to bring home. And life goes on – as we were to discover even more cruelly later with Jack. No matter what tragedies surround you, bills still have to be paid and businesses run. And so Mary-Ann carried on growing Lily O'Brien's. Because she was breast-feeding Phonsie, he had to come along every day in his Moses basket with her to the Phoenix Park, where he was popped into one of the huge old ovens – not lit, obviously, and with the door open – a safe, convenient but unorthodox place for him. There was an old food lift, one of those cranky, creaky old things, that ran from the kitchens up to the executive suites, that had fed the directors and big clients in the days of fancy lunches. There was also a health and safety officer who came round occasionally to check up on the production, so a sort of tom-tom drum evolved. As soon as she was spotted, the warning cry would go up – 'Mayday, Mayday' – and Phonsie, in his little basket, would be put in the dumb waiter and shot up to the executive suite. It worked wonderfully, and no one ever found out Mary-Ann had a baby on the premises.

However, Mary-Ann quickly outgrew the Phoenix Park, brought in Peter Queally and Dawn Farms as a partner and moved into one of their factories in Naas. That was the real jump, from cottage industry to serious contender. The first day we walked in we thought, 'God, you'd fit a jumbo jet in here. We'll be rattling around like dried peas …' Within eighteen months there was no more room for further expansion, at which stage Mary-Ann moved to the Industrial Development in Ireland Agency (IDA) business park in Newbridge, into a factory at least double the size of the Dawn Farms one, at which stage the evolution of Lily O'Brien's, from teeny-tiny farmer's market staple into a major player, was truly complete.

In 2011 Mary-Ann got a call from Taoiseach Enda Kenny, asking her to take up a position in Seanad Éireann. Because she felt this was an opportunity to provide a voice for those who can't speak up for themselves and use her position to generate more debate on the economy and jobs, Mary-Ann agreed, and has since had a track record of action on matters as diverse as pardons for Irish soldiers who deserted during the Second World War to join the British Army and fight fascism, and the very real dangers of social media for teenagers. Her motivation in every case is a sense of injustice, or an understanding of ways in which ordinary people's lives can be improved and safeguarded.

11

JACK

Jack was born on 29 February 1996, about two years after the twins. It was a difficult birth, but he was a fine, healthy baby, weighing a whopping 12 lbs, with a huge head of hair and utterly beautiful. Mary-Ann and I thought we had won the lottery. He was slightly mucus-y, as so many babies are, but nothing that anyone was concerned about. We sent news to family and friends that mother and son were doing well – one friend, Wendy Reynolds, who later helped me so much in setting up the Jack and Jill Foundation, remembers getting a call from Mary-Ann, who said about Jack, then a few hours old, 'He's great. He's just gone down the road with my dad for a pint in the Shelbourne.'

On the second night of Jack's life, staff in Holles Street suggested to Mary-Ann that they take him down to the nursery so she could get some sleep because she was ready to be discharged the next day. They promised to bring him back when he needed to be fed. That was the last time Mary-Ann saw Jack as a healthy infant.

She was woken up at about 1 a.m. and told that Jack was in intensive care, that there was a problem. The most terrifying words in the world to a new mother. She ran to the Intensive Care Unit (ICU), where she found her baby, our darling Jack, smothered with tubes. At first she thought she was having a nightmare, but alas it was all too real. Jack had some kind of crisis in the night, had most probably died and been resuscitated, but not before oxygen starvation had permanently damaged his brain.

As far as we know and understand any of what happened – which even now is not the full picture – Jack choked on his own mucus and died in his cot before anyone found him. The members of staff were overworked, there were a lot of babies in the nursery that night and they don't routinely have monitors on them, so they knew nothing until it was too late. By the time he was resuscitated, Jack's brain was destroyed. In a way, and I will always feel this, despite the many good things that have come out of Jack's life and death, I still feel that it is a pity he was brought back to life. From that moment on his life was so very difficult and painful. He couldn't swallow and so by the time Mary-Ann reached the nursery that night, he already had a tube up his nose, through which he was fed, and was in great pain.

We got back the baby that no family wants to get back, no matter how much they love him or her. Those were really among the darkest moments of my life. Jack was severely brain-damaged, couldn't swallow, couldn't hear, we suspected he couldn't see either, but the first appointment to get his eyes tested was twenty-one months down the line. In fact, we never did get his eyes or ears tested, because he died before that time came. He had constant epileptic fits until heavy medication brought that under some kind of control, but that left him heavily drugged. He was in constant pain and cried all the time, an endless, heart-breaking wail that we couldn't soothe or quiet, and that tore at our already shredded nerves. No matter how much we loved him, we couldn't make his life easier for him, couldn't calm his distress, and knowing that made everything so much worse.

Jack stayed in intensive care for four weeks. We were constantly warned that it was very unlikely that he would make it. Even with tube feeding, staff had great trouble getting any sustenance into him, mucus was constantly building up, and we were permanently on tenterhooks, expecting him to die. But he battled on. Mary-Ann and I would go up together and visit him, sitting beside his cot, talking to him, doing what we could and trying to learn from the staff what his needs were. The ICU of a maternity hospital is a terribly sad place, full of broken dreams and devastated hopes. We got to know many parents who, like us, were there for the long term. Many of them had come up with their babies from the countryside and were trying to care for their sick babies a long way from home. They often had other children who also needed to be looked after, but who had been left behind to be cared for by friends and relatives. We had Lily and Phonsie, both still very young, at home to mind, but at least we were within daily driving distance of the hospital. The logistical difficulties, on top of the emotional trauma, of the lives of those parents made a great impression on both Mary-Ann and me.

After the ICU, Jack was moved to the neo-natal unit for two months. There, too, there was definitely a feeling among the staff, kind as they were, that he was a no-hoper. We rang everyone we knew who had the slightest connection to medicine, all the contacts we had in the world, and it became very apparent there was no solution to Jack's problems. There was no swimming with dolphins, no wonder-drug, no miracle that could cure him.

No one ever actually said, 'You have to leave; there is nothing we can do for this child,' but we did realise after a while that he couldn't stay in the neo-natal unit at Holles Street. Once we realised it was time to bring Jack home, we asked to see the senior paediatrician, a very fine man, to try to work out what we needed to do next with this baby who needed so much more support than we were prepared for.

In the paediatrician's office I said, 'We desperately need a route map for what to do from here, where to go for the help we need.' To which the paediatrician answered, 'Sit down both of you, because this is a much worse tragedy than you can imagine.'

Until this point, no one had indicated, not by the flicker of an eyelid, that there was a further, major problem. We presumed there was a system in place to help us care for Jack, because obviously he wasn't the first poor little baby to need it. We believed that we would leave the hospital and tap into the available resources to help us care for this child and give him the best quality of life possible. But there, in that office, the paediatrician told us, 'I hate to tell you, but once you leave here, in the year 1996 in this very prosperous country, there are no services whatsoever for your son. You are basically being sent home with Jack, for him to die in your arms at some point down the line. You probably don't understand what a burden you have, because while this little fellow would love you like any baby would love their parents, unfortunately, every hour of your and his life is going to be a struggle. He cries twenty-four hours a day, it takes eighteen hours a day to feed him through the tube in his nose, which causes him immense distress. You both have jobs, and knowing the world we live in you will have to keep your jobs, because although your baby is sick, bills will still keep flopping in the front door. The strain will be enormous on you. It will probably break your marriage up – that wouldn't be unusual – and it will certainly ruin the childhood of Jack's brother and sister.'

Those were his words, paraphrased now by me, but the essence of them is unchanged. He spelled out for us – in the bleakest possible way, no sugar-coating whatsoever, the future that lay before our family. I am still grateful to him for his absolute, searing honesty, but the shock of hearing what he had to say, on top of the barely assimilated shock of Jack's condition, was the most overwhelming thing you can imagine. When he said that Lily and Phonsie's childhoods would be ruined by the needs of their baby brother, that was a bitter, unbearable blow. Not only was our darling Jack's life destroyed, now his siblings would suffer too.

Even while we were struggling to make sense of what he had said, the paediatrician went on: 'I can't get you out of this in a humane way. There is a pathway out, but it is brutal.'

And he laid it before us, apparently the only solution to our problems: 'What you do is, you take him home, see how you get on, but the results won't be good. After a while, when you realise that you can no longer cope – in a few weeks or maybe a few months – repack his little bag, drive him up to Crumlin, because it's the closest children's hospital to you, get him admitted, but do so knowing that you're going to walk away and abandon him. And when I say abandon him, I mean do so knowing that you can never go back to see him. That will put a gun to the head of the health service; only once they realise that you have abandoned Jack will they actually step forward and have to look after him.'

That was the only possible solution that this clever, honest and decent man could see to our problems. To simply abandon our baby.

Society was talking in shocked terms about the state of orphanages in Romania, in China and in Russia. Yet this was Ireland in the 1990s, and that was the only option open to us as parents of a child with profound disabilities. To walk away from Jack, turn our backs and somehow struggle along with our own lives, knowing that we had taken from him the only thing he would ever really have – his parents' love. There must be other parents throughout the country who made that decision, had it forced upon them by the shocking neglect of a government who preferred to pretend these vulnerable little babies didn't exist. Those parents will have spent the rest of their lives living with the horror and guilt of what they were forced to do. Mary-Ann and I may well have ended up among them, if it hadn't been for a remarkable, wonderful series of quite unexpected events.

We did go home, and we brought Jack with us. We had no plan, except to try to cope somehow. I was running the Dublin Sports Council at the time, and Mary-Ann was running her business, Lily O'Brien's, having recently moved to the huge purpose-built factory in Naas where she employed forty people and was steadily growing a very successful brand. Our world had changed completely. In a way it felt like it was standing still, despite the frantic attempts to keep up with Jack's needs, but around us, life moved on. You cannot close a factory and put forty people out of work because the boss's son is sick; you just can't. So Mary-Ann was struggling to manage the factory as well as Jack. I had my job in Dublin and was going up and back every day. Between us, we managed for about three months. Mary-Ann was crying most of the time, she was so exhausted, and the other two children were being very much neglected, just as the paediatrician had predicted they would be. It took almost twenty-two hours a day to tube-feed Jack, because he needed to be fed minuscule drop by minuscule drop of milk. Any more and he would throw up. He already had huge problems breathing, and throwing up made that much worse. He carried on having daily epileptic fits and couldn't be fed during or immediately after one of these fits. He didn't really sleep, just cat-napped here and there for maybe half an hour at a time. Certainly there was no question of Mary-Ann and I going to bed for the night, although we would give each other a few hours whenever we could.

There was no fun, no games in the lives of Lily and Phonsie, no outings, very little parental attention. Everything we had was going into trying to care for Jack, and these babies are not easy to look after. He was in pain the whole time and on drugs the whole time. He was frequently sick, on top of his existing problems, because these babies get everything; if there's a sniffle in the village, they get full-blown flu. When that happened, we would have to take him up to Crumlin Hospital, which was added strain on an already impossible situation, and where we quickly realised that services for the parents of very sick children were non-existent. The nights we spent there with Jack, one or other of us would have to sleep, or try to, on the floor under his little bed, and then get up and go to work the next day and try to function as normal. Since then, Ronald McDonald House has opened and the situation is better, but in those days it was dire. Anyway, Crumlin wasn't the right place for a baby like Jack, who needed constant care and holding. The staff simply didn't have time for him. Nor was he able to fight the infections that hospitals are full of. The first time he went in, he got MRSA and pneumonia within two days and we had to bring him home. That meant going over every single inch of the house with a steam cleaner before he came back, in case he contracted something else.

Nature is horrid; babies like Jack become epileptic and all their limbs start twisting like olive branches, but of course there was no paediatric physiotherapy in those days to help him. He was in more pain and distress with every week that passed, just as we were becoming more ragged with exhaustion. He had regular seizures, needed constant postural drainage, reflux operations and suctioning.

We were trying to cope through a muggy haze, because we got very little sleep, rarely more than an hour or two a night. We were also living in guilt – should you stay at home or go to work? Should you be in the hospital or with the other children? Could you go to the school play, but who would stay with Jack? I think the lowest point – and there were many, many low moments – came one morning at breakfast, when Mary-Ann couldn't physically get out of her chair. She seemed catatonic, she was in a wretched way, so traumatised and sleep-deprived that she simply wasn't functioning at all any more.

But then a most extraordinary thing happened. Something that showed me there is so much good in the world, so much kindness among the ordinary people of this country. Around that time Norah Byrne, a lady who worked in the Lily O'Brien factory, came off the packing line, went to Mary-Ann and said, 'I know about the tragedy you have with your little son. I was a nurse until I got married. Could I see if I could possibly help?'

Until that point, we had had no help. Literally, none. We existed alone in a kind of parallel universe with our sick baby, and no one was there to help. The public health nurse would come once a week – she was very pleasant and would come in, have a cup of tea and maybe weigh Phonsie. But in those days, no health nurses were trained in paediatrics and so, although she was nice, there was little she could do for us. After her cup of tea she would go away and there would be twenty-three-and-a-half hours left in that day, and another six more days in the week, and thirty more days in the month, and on and on into the future with no respite, no hope of improvement and no peace for this poor child.

So along came Norah Byrne, and she got on with Jack like a house on fire. She understood him, she knew what needed to be done for him – the first thing she did was run a bath and put in a few drops of lavender oil. She knew that warm water would soothe his poor, contorted limbs, like the branches of a small, stunted tree, and indeed he calmed down almost immediately he was put into the bath. That was the one place he was relatively happy and relatively free from pain, so that is where Norah would feed him. A simple thing, but one that made an immense difference to his life, and to ours. The other thing he liked, that quietened him, was to walk him around the garden on a sunny day, so that he could sense the pattern of leaves playing across his face.

Around the same time, Jack's godfather, Richard Butler, my wonderful 'feud' from Stonehouse and Eton, came over from London and gave us an envelope with £5,000 in it, to help with minding Jack.

Looking back, it seems to me that from that moment on, life began to change. People started knocking at our door, sometimes people we didn't know and who didn't know us, but who lived locally and had heard about our tragedy. They all said, 'We've come to see if we can help you.' Some just wanted to hold the baby while Mary-Ann had a shower, or do the hoovering for her, but some were trained nurses and, like Norah Byrne, knew what to do for Jack. Thanks to Richard's extraordinary gift, we could pay these women – Teresa Moore, Imelda Whelan, Anne O'Brien, Eva Breen, Lila McGee and Kathleen Livingston – something for their help. Gradually, the light and laughter began to come back into the house.

For the remaining eighteen months of Jack's life, he was basically nursed around the clock by an extraordinary band of six amazing women. Once he was minded properly, we started to see a real difference in him. He started to laugh, to recognise us. And shared between six people, the minding became a joy rather than a chore. The change in all of our lives was just unbelievable. Mary-Ann and I got some rest and respite, Lily and Phonsie were able to spend time with us again, to do simple things with us that had been impossible for months – we could take them into school in the mornings ourselves, rather than leaving it to a friend or family member – and even though there was always a black dog there, a weight of depression and sadness, and we knew it, we were calm, we could function. Lily and Phonsie began to enjoy their little brother – they had a game where they would wrap a silk scarf around his neck and put him propped up in a cardboard box in the kitchen, then get a hair dryer and blow warm air into his face, so the scarf streamed out behind him, pretending that he was in a sports car. And each of the six women who minded Jack fell in love with him and became his mother. That care and love are what the Jack and Jill Foundation has tried to replicate all over Ireland.

The first time Jack laughed was one Saturday morning. He was in the arms of his favourite nurse, Teresa Moore – he loved them all, but she was the boldest and he seemed to have a particular affection for her. She smoked and played poker and was a great gambler. For big races, she'd always have a bet on, for herself and for Jack. That Saturday, the Aintree Grand National was scheduled, but the IRA had put a bomb somewhere near the course and there were police everywhere, with all sorts of men wearing trilby hats coming on TV to say how absolutely disgraceful it all was. For some unknown reason, Jack broke into peals of laughter. It was as if he had some sense of the chaos going on and it appealed to him. That was one of the highlights of his short life and to us like church bells on Christmas morning, because he had never laughed before.

Jack died on 13 December 1997, strangely, the date of my father's birthday. It was a quiet, sunny Saturday morning. Mary-Ann had gone out to the post office and he just slipped away in the arms of the same favourite nurse. It was unexpected, because he was quite well at the time. He had just had his bath, was tucked up in Teresa's arms, and he just went, so quietly. I think these little people don't want to die while their parents are there. I have seen it since, many times. It's as if it is easier for them to slip away when no one is watching.

He is buried alongside his brother John, in the tiny graveyard at Ballinure. The day of his funeral the church was overflowing, with people standing right through the church yard to say goodbye to this little boy that many of them had never even met. That second time of putting a little white coffin into the ground was almost too much to bear.

We were heartbroken. We didn't think he was going to die. We had talked about our long-term life, planning for the day we wouldn't be able to lift him, that he would need the house adapted to suit him. He smelled so beautiful and was such a smasher, but I also know that he is better off where he is. For Jack, I believe death was a blessing, because his life on this earth as we know it was dreadful and would probably only have got worse. The constant pain he suffered would not have let up, the complications around his condition would probably have got worse, and the difficulties of permanently caring for a six-, seven-, eight-year-old, let alone a teenager or fully-grown adult, are so much greater than for a tiny baby.

After his death, Mary-Ann and I looked at each other and we swore that no family with a baby like Jack would ever go through what we had been through on their own again; it just wasn't to be tolerated. And we stuck to that promise, for all the families who found themselves in terrible despair just as we had, and who didn't have a godfather from London to walk in the door with £5,000.

Jack came down here to do a job. He taught his parents a few lessons and showed them what is important. The passion that was ignited by that little baby has never diminished. Out of his painful, tragic life and untimely death has come enormous good.

12

JACK AND JILL

The twenty-two months of Jack's life took Mary-Ann and me out of the rather charmed world we had inhabited and threw us into a very different reality. Before Jack, although we had known hard times, particularly during my divorce, when Mary-Ann had ME and the terrible loss of John, we had not known such constant pain. We had never been forced to imagine the lives of people in great need of support, for whom there is no assistance readily provided. All of that we learned through Jack: the heartbreak that comes with being told your baby will never be well and the relentless exhaustion of trying to care for an infant with severe disabilities in a state that prefers to pretend that such children do not exist.

We got to see and understand at first hand the indifference with which Official Ireland treated the smallest and most vulnerable of its citizens. I still genuinely believe that the state, in as much as it considered these children at all, just presumed they would not survive infancy, and that four years of age was time enough to begin to provide services to them, if indeed they lived that long. Their only strategy at that time seemed to be to send the mother home with her baby for it to die in her arms six weeks or six months later. It was a strategy that looked like it was dreamed up during the days of large Irish families, who would all muck in and help out: the kind of family the writer Christy Brown, who had severe cerebral palsy from birth, was lucky enough to have, but hardly the kind of firm basis on which to plan for the care of very vulnerable children. Basically, the government just hoped the problems would go away.

Despite the many problems with Jack's health, and the fact that he was in almost constant need of medical help, he had no automatic entitlement to a medical card. In fact, this was initially turned down on the basis that our financial circumstances didn't qualify him, and it was only when I personally rang Charlie McCreevy, our local TD, that a medical card was speedily granted to Jack. That is wrong, very wrong. The system, such as it was, worked in our favour because we knew someone who could help us, could make a call and get the state decision overturned. It shouldn't be like that. The system should work fairly for everyone, not just those with connections. And I strongly believe, have always believed, that children with such profound disabilities as Jack should be entitled to medical cards regardless of their parents' salaries. I don't understand why children aren't considered as individuals in their own right before the age of sixteen. There is no other section of the community where the state insists on a third party becoming involved: the medical card isn't for the family, it's for the child. Every step and stage of Jack's life showed us the appalling limitations of the state, and the consequent tremendous difficulties faced by the parents and families of these children. We were lucky because we had a big comfortable house, some money, a wide circle of family and friends, and so we could cope, just about. Matters are very different for families living on limited incomes, more socially isolated.

The wonderful women who came into our lives and took care of Jack showed us how it could be done, how beautifully these babies could be looked after, how your household could return to some semblance of normality and your other children be granted some of the attention they badly needed. And that was what Mary-Ann and I resolved to do: to take that model that we had tried and tested and bring it to other families who needed it. It was a simple idea, a simple resolution, born of hard experience. We have travelled a long way since then, but the essence of what we want to do has never changed: to soften the blow that having a child like Jack inevitably is in anyone's life; to spare these parents some of the pain and misery that is their lot; to advocate on their behalf for better than the state is willing to provide.

Mary-Ann was incredibly busy with Lily O'Brien's by then, but I had reached a stage in my life where I was ready for a change, and where I felt so strongly about what we had been through that I knew I could not rest until I knew there was something in place for other Jacks, and Jills, out there. And of course, a sense of purpose helped to fill the hole that was left by Jack's death. Not only had his physical care taken up a great part of our lives, so that for a short while we almost wondered what to do with ourselves in those spare hours, but the sense of grief and frustration at the short span of his life, the constant pain he suffered and the never-ending disbelief that a healthy, bonny baby could have developed such profound disabilities in the space of one terrible night, all of these things were helped by having a purpose and a mission to complete.

At fifty-five, I didn't have a career that anyone could threaten and I wasn't intimidated by anyone. I had the contacts, the experience and the willpower to push ahead. If I had been twenty-three or twenty-four when Jack was born, the Jack and Jill Foundation wouldn't exist. I wouldn't have had the wherewithal to make it happen. I am distraught at Jack's short life and death, but amazed by what has come out of it.

The other thing that helped after Jack's death was that although I firmly believe the hospital were very much at fault in what happened and even though everyone was saying, 'Sue, sue, sue', and we got as far as retaining doctors and solicitors and barristers, we decided not to. I remember thinking, if we go through with this, then in two years time, on the steps of the court, the hospital will probably settle with us on the basis that they don't have to admit fault and anything they give us will feel like blood money.

I think that decision to walk away is one of the luckiest things that ever happened to us. Certainly, it saved me from becoming crabby and bitter and twisted, wrapped up in the outcome of the case, living for the conflict. If I had chosen the other route, I would, I am certain, have become like an old conker soaked in vinegar, like the ones we used to play with in school – hard, wrinkled, shrivelled. Instead, Mary-Ann and I decided to go the positive way.

I never think, 'Isn't it wonderful that Jack should have been afflicted as he was,' but it is a source of enormous pleasure that the things done in his name have worked so well. I don't see myself as any better a person than I was before, and I certainly don't blame any parent who decides to pursue the legal route. When I see a case concerning a child like Jack has been settled, and a pay-out has been made, my first questions is always – was that child on our books? And if the answer is no, and sometimes it still is no, I feel a bit sad about that, because I know the difference we could have made to their lives. I'm always shocked by the length of time the parents have to fight to get the hospital into court, the amount of energy that is put into resisting them, with so little thought for the added heartache and distress this causes the family. I notice more and more that the judges are picking the defendants up on this point.

A big factor in our decision not to go down the legal route was that Jack died so terribly young. However hard caring for a tiny baby who has round-the-clock needs is, caring for a fully-grown adult with the same needs, when you yourself are getting older and more feeble, is a whole different game. In that situation the need for money to ensure their future is overwhelming. But for Mary-Ann and me, the decision not to sue was the right one. Instead, we created the Jack and Jill Foundation.

The name came about from the old nursery rhyme: 'Jack and Jill went up the hill, to fetch a pail of water. Jack fell down and broke his crown, and Jill came tumbling after.' I immediately thought of it – I don't know why – when we were looking for a name, I suppose because I associated 'broke his crown' with brain damage. I still think that was a great coup, getting the name so very right. There are so many charities in Ireland – 24,000 was a recent estimate, of which 800 are registered. Many have very obscure names; the label just doesn't tell you what you're buying. The Jack and Jill Children's Foundation is wonderfully clear and evocative, and I think that has helped us. It certainly helped people to remember that we existed, in the very early days. I would go on radio and talk about the Foundation, and explain the kind of help we could give to families, and the name stuck in people's minds because it almost told a little story in itself.

The Foundation offers home respite care to severely disabled children and their families all over Ireland and also acts as an advocate for families in helping secure a carer's allowance, a medical card, correct housing, special equipment or a primary medical certificate. Our criteria are as straightforward as we can make them. The nub of our kernel is brain damage, because that requires twenty-four-hour nursing. We don't take on children with spina bifida, for example, or with Down's syndrome, unless that child has other complications that bring him or her into our area, because they don't require the same level of intensity of care. It is very difficult when you get a family on the phone asking for help that we can't give because their child doesn't fit our parameters. We have a high proportion of people coming here to make lives for themselves, from as far afield as Egypt and Syria for example, who have no family back-up. Their child may be unwell, with sight problems, or hearing problems, but they don't fit our criteria, yet the public health nurses refer them automatically to us because they have nothing else to offer these desperate parents. That is very hard to turn your back on, and yet we must. Unless we keep our focus, keep our sights on the children we set out to help, we will be impossibly swamped.

We have never turned our backs on a baby who meets our criteria, no matter how stretched our resources, and so the number of children we were helping gradually grew from five, to twelve, to twenty. We broke the 100 mark and now have around 300 children in our care at any one time. We look after these children until they are four years old. We had to put a ceiling on it, because otherwise it would have been impossible to begin to calculate financial projections, and at age four the state is supposed to step in, although very often not as fully as is required and in reality we would never cut off our help from a child who still needs it. We couldn't do that. Tragically, many of our children don't make it to that age and there have been many, many funerals over the years, but for those who do, we continue to supplement the state's support with our own care.

Now, I'll be totally honest: when I started on this journey I thought I would have a little office somewhere, with a wonderful woman in it running things, and that once we were up and running, I would simply drop in every Friday and say, 'How's it all going? How are the babies?' That sort of stuff. I really didn't realise that this was going to be a seven-days-a-week, eating, sleeping, waking type of undertaking. If I had known, who can say what I would have done, but I didn't, and perhaps it's just as well.

13

BABY STEPS

The first thing, of course, was to raise some money. Now, I was very lucky I'd had thirty-five great years in the horse racing industry; I understood marketing and branding very well, and I knew the value of theatre and a certain kind of showmanship. I knew I could get money for these babies. And indeed, people proved to be incredibly generous. We held golf classics – the first, through Mary-Ann's father, Phonsie O'Brien, at Mount Juliet, raised a stunning £64,000 – and marathons – the target for our first women's mini marathon was close to £20,000.

The first person I employed was Wendy Reynolds, without whom none of this would have been remotely possible. She approached the Sobell Foundation in England, who help in the setting up of charities, to look for sponsorship for the Foundation's administration costs, because she knew very well that anyone who is going to donate money to a charity wants to know that their donation is going straight to help the needy and not into the cost of running an office. So in November 1997, the Sobell Foundation donated £25,000 sterling, with a further grant of £25,000 sterling the following year.

Tony Ryan was a friend of mine, but I had only worked as

marketing director for Ryanair for a short time; nevertheless, he sent me an amazing cheque when we first started, completely out of the blue. Thereafter, when members of the public went to visit his wonderful house, Lyons Demesne, all the revenue from their contributions was given to Jack and Jill, and he also left leaflets around the house. Other private donations came in too, bringing that figure to £62,000, making the income for our first year around £170,000. Our outgoings, for that first year, were £117,000.

By hook or by crook, we got the money together and set off on this incredible journey. We got charitable status from the Revenue. I bullied some friends to become trustees: Sir Richard Butler, Nicholas Cowan, Tom Donohoe, Michael Fitzgerald, Tony Hanahoe, Dr Ann Heffernan, Mark Kavanagh, Philip Lynch, Lee Mallaghan (our former landlord in the Carton House apartment), Colette Morrissey, Peter Murray, Gillian O'Brien, Robin O'Reilly (then married to Tony O'Reilly Jnr), Peter Queally, Susan Sangster and Sharon Smurfit. Why those particular people? Because I knew they had big-enough hearts not to be able to refuse me when I asked.

At the first meeting the trustees said, 'So what will we do? Look after two or three babies?' I remember feeling just like I imagine Lord Nelson did at the battle of Copenhagen, when Admiral Sir Hyde Parker told him to keep a spyglass trained on his signals and withdraw on command. Nelson put the telescope to his rotten eye so he couldn't see a thing and just kept on battling. Rather like that, I set off with these poor trustees in a big fat cart behind me, going goodness knows where, because at that time, to be perfectly honest, I had no idea how many babies like Jack there were in the country. There could have been ten, there could have been 1,000. I just knew that we needed to find out, and that we would never turn a baby away.

The problem was that the state health boards had no idea how many babies like Jack were out there. There was no database at all; it was as if the children didn't exist. Even now, sixteen years later, I don't believe disabled children under the age of six are really on the state radar at all. Slightly more now, because we've made so much noise, but still not nearly enough.

We needed a much clearer picture of the situation and what was required in terms of resources, and so we commissioned our own research from the Graduate School of Business at UCD. They were asked to raise a profile on existing services and information available for children with special needs. They found the situation to be as bleak as Mary-Ann and I had discovered. Looking back over the document we produced to outline the purpose and aims of the Jack and Jill Foundation, I see that the report:

> ... identified a gap in the State Health Services which precludes either homecare or respite support until the child reaches four years of age. The parents and siblings of these children are placed under intolerable strain, experiencing great distress and a sense of loneliness with no expectations of support either financial or physical. The Foundation was created to raise sufficient funds to redress this devastating situation for the parents within the 26 Counties.

We also discovered that families who were able to access some services had to fight tooth and nail for every single thing they got, just as we had, and – most shamefully – that the more modest the family circumstances were, the more indifference they received at the hands of the officers of the state. Basically, if they didn't know someone in a position of some power who would reach out, usually going over the heads of the civil servants, they received almost no help. It was that brutal, and that simple. And we discovered a huge geographical disparity, which still exists, in what was on offer. Even now, I could tell you where are the best places in this country to give birth to a child with disabilities and the black spots where services are worse than minimal.

As I embarked on this journey to help families and children like Jack, I met an awful lot of Eastern Health Board officials, as they were then. They were generally very nice to me, but clearly didn't take what I was saying at all seriously. After one meeting that I had felt had gone rather well, I heard on the grapevine that this particular official had said, 'Oh, just another of those grieving fathers with ideas that will never come to anything.'

That was very much the way we were treated at first and, in fairness to them, a lot of the time that is a fair assessment; motivated by grief, people begin trying to do something to help, but quickly, because the barriers are so great, the walls thrown up by the established services are so huge, they become daunted and give up. I think this is why there are so very many charities in the country. Each one has behind it a terrible tragedy, a loss for some family, who, in their grief, wish to reach out and help others. Except that it is never as easy to help as one might think it will be, and the obstacles to accomplishing anything substantial are too great.

I was determined that wouldn't be my story. And I had many years' experience of getting ideas up and running, often in the teeth of indifference and even opposition, which meant I was reasonably able for the sometimes depressing official attitude. The Foundation began life in an office in Merrion Square – so tiny that Wendy Reynolds remembers that she used to bring in a laptop and a deck chair for herself, and squeeze into whatever space was available between the other desks. When it came to putting a telephone number on our fancy headed paper, Wendy and I were totally stumped, because neither of us was full-time with the Foundation by then – we both had other jobs – and this was pre-mobile phones of course. In the end we put Wendy's home number at the Ballymacoll Stud, because her husband Peter managed the farm, so at least we knew there would be someone there to answer the phone.

From there we moved to a small office in Ellenborough House in Naas, and later to the larger premises in Johnstown which we still occupy. The building wasn't fully built, only the external walls and basic internal structure had been put together; I presumed we needed an architect to map out the interior of our floor, but Wendy and Tracy Marsden wouldn't hear of incurring such unnecessary expense. They came in one Sunday and started moving blocks of wood around, pacing out the rooms and marking the spaces. By 4 p.m. they had it all laid out and that Monday they met the builders and said, 'Right, just follow the plans as marked by our blocks of wood.'

In October 1997 our first family came on board, followed by the second in December. Both of those were through word of mouth, and initially all we were able to do was listen in sympathy and provide money for the care their children needed. We didn't then have the kind of structure that would allow us to intervene any further.

Looking back at the case notes of some of the babies we had in the early days tells so much of our story. One little boy, who I am going to call Paul, was diagnosed as having 'quadriplegic cerebral palsy, secondary to severe birth asphyxia, epilepsy, profound learning difficulties, scoliosis, and generalised osteoporosis'. Our case notes show that:

[Paul] wakes frequently during the night and requires turning in bed. Can often be unsettled both day and night. Suffers from frequent hospital admissions especially in winter due to chestiness. Also has the occasional seizure. Paul makes some attempts at vocalisation when spoken to and will smile. Loves family interaction, especially that of his siblings. Loves music. Paul loves to be held and talked to, also reacts to tactile stimulation. Eyesight to be assessed later. He is fed via gastrostomy tube all the time due to his severe gastro-oesophageal reflux. Suffers from constipation due to his condition and also his immobility. He is able to turn his head slowly. Otherwise, he has very little mobility. Paul wears a back brace twenty-four hours a day due to his scoliosis and leg splints due to osteoporosis. He is also on antispasmodics.

Paul's family circumstances are also carefully laid out:

> Paul's dad has just started a new office job. Mum is at home full-time with the four children. Both parents are often exhausted due to frequent sleepless nights and have little time to spend with the other children. Mum needs practical hands-on help with Paul. Parents also need time out together and in their absence a qualified nurse is required.

Just reading those notes gives a picture of the lives of this particular family. The stress and strain, the exhaustion and impossibility of coping with all these demands on their own. The pitiful conditions that Paul suffered from, coupled with the loving nature of any child, his joy at family interaction and interest in music. The estimated cost to the Jack and Jill Foundation of providing assistance to this family in such dire need was £150 a week.

Another case, this time concerning twins, was of two boys diagnosed at five months with chronic epilepsy, febrile related and chromosomal.

> Both boys sleep in cots either side of mum's bed and often vomit and take seizures during sleep. Both have breathing difficulties during more severe seizures and require oxygen and suctioning during seizures. They both also suffer from bronchiolitis. These boys love to play but are often unable to do so due to seizures. Safety during play is so important and therefore they cannot be let out of sight. They are very happy, outgoing boys when well.

They love games and music but their concentration span is very short and deteriorating. Both boys eat and drink well when awake and will spoon feed. Sometimes very difficult to get adequate nutrition when drowsy post seizures and frequently require IV fluids. Both boys were crawling well but this has now stopped due to increased seizures. Activity helmets have been ordered to protect the head during seizure episodes. Mum has few available supporters to assist her with the on-going, demanding nature of the twins' medical condition. She receives Lone Parents Allowance and gets a small contribution from dad. Hospital appointment, physiotherapy, shopping, etc., prove very difficult as the twins often have seizures simultaneously. They are currently in hospital. Prognosis is uncertain. Due to the severity of the boys' condition, mum needs some practical hands-on help with them by a paediatric nurse. Social Worker has also asked for help in the purchase of a car to alleviate travel difficulties.

Here, the story is of a woman coping alone, and without much help, with her sons' conditions that appear to be degenerating. The report talks of reduced mobility, increased seizures and dependency. Reading between the lines, it is not hard to piece together a tale of despair and to see that a great deal of help and support is required if she and her children are to reach a decent level of comfort and ease. The estimated cost to the Foundation of helping that family was £100 a week, plus a contribution towards the cost of the car.

Yet another case concerns a girl, who I will call Sarah, who was diagnosed as having microcephaly with quadriplegic cerebral palsy.

Sarah suffers from intractable seizures, which make her irritable and difficult to manage. She also has frequent chest infections, which require high-dose antibiotics and hospital admissions. Sarah wakes frequently at night especially when sick and is very difficult to settle. She also sleeps very little during the day and is often irritable, especially after a seizure. Sarah has frequent apnoea episodes especially during seizures and requires home oxygen therapy. Sarah likes music and noisy toys. She is unable to hold or manipulate toys herself. She loves sitting in front of the television especially when *Teletubbies* are on. Sarah is unable to speak and requires one-to-one stimulation and attention. She does have some hearing and sight and is to have further assessments shortly. She loves interacting with people when well and responds in her own way to the attention. Sarah has a gastrostomy tube for all her dietary requirements due to the high risk of aspiration with oral feeding. Sarah is quadriplegic and therefore has very limited movement. She also has severe hypertonia, which makes positioning extremely difficult. She also has very poor head control. Sarah's mother Claire [name changed] is a lone parent. Her father is involved and supportive but lives with his wife and family. The County Council has recently housed Sarah and her mother. Claire is doing a FÁS course for a few hours each morning and hopes to get a job when she finishes. Sarah goes to a normal crèche while mum is working and Claire is getting some assistance with the cost of this. The crèche is, however, not able to provide a specialised programme for Sarah or even give her one-to-one attention. Our recommendations are that Claire needs to get out with her friends occasionally and requires an experienced person to look after Sarah and to provide her with appropriate stimulation.

This is a story of a woman trying to educate and better herself, while struggling to cope with a child with profound disabilities, who requires almost constant attention.

Without the intervention of the Jack and Jill Foundation, all of these people – the children, their parents and families – would have been left to cope as best they could, largely alone and without help from the state. One very crucial distinction between Jack and Jill and the state, is that we always saw the personality of the child, their likes and dislikes, the things that interested them. To us, they were and are children first, in need of help second. For the health boards and their successor the Health Service Executive (HSE) too often they were simply unsolvable problems.

Just handing over money was never the extent of our plan – we were determined to help nurse these children and to provide comfort in the lives of their parents. To do that, I needed an experienced nurse to be the manager and co-ordinator of that side of things. That's when I met Mary Joe Guilfoyle, who is either mad, or one of the most extraordinary people I've ever met in my life. Probably both. I needed a nurse, as I clearly couldn't nurse the babies, so I advertised and Mary Joe turned up for an interview in the basement of the Alexander Hotel in Dublin. At the time she was part of the senior nursing staff at Temple Street Children's Hospital. I related my tale and told her what it was that I was going to do. At that point I am still astonished that she didn't say, 'I'm so sorry for your troubles, but this will never happen and I'm not willing to be part of it.' Instead she went away to think about what I had said, rang back the next day and said, 'I'm yours,' and is with me to this day. Right from the start she gave a tranquillity and professionalism to the Jack and Jill Foundation. She is a very warm person, but has fortitude and character. If parents need help with the HSE, she is there, and she won't take no for an answer. Calmly, persistently, she will fight the parents' battles for them, one step at a time. The other nurses, as they came along, were of the same mould, and only two have ever left us, both times for reasons beyond their control. We have twelve liaison nurses now, who each look after a particular geographic region.

I was always going to try and tread the national stage, because that's my nature. When I spoke on the radio in the early days, talking about what it was I wished to do, we used to get a few cheques, kind donations, which was wonderful, but one of the best feelings of all was when we got a note or a telephone call or an email from somebody who'd never heard of us before, saying, 'I think my baby, my grandchild, my nephew, might be a Jack and Jill child.' By spreading the word, we gradually gathered all the babies together under our wing, and I would hope that there is nobody now in the country who wouldn't, if that tragic situation came about in their lives, know instantly to contact Jack and Jill. Because once they get hold of us, we are waiting on the doorstep when you bring your child home from hospital, ready to implement the same system of constant care that Mary-Ann and I learned with Jack.

At first I did think about raising money to provide residential care for Jack and Jill children, but for various reasons we decided against this. First, because I think it is happier for everyone if these children are nursed in their own homes. I think home is where children reach their maximum potential, even if they are still damaged. And it is happier for the mother, even if it does mean the dog charging into the room, or the other children jumping around and shouting. Acute hospitals are not for Jack and Jill children. They are good for appendicitis, burns, broken legs, but they don't have time to hold the babies, and children like Jack need to be held for as long as possible. Also, I think that although Phonsie doesn't remember all that much about Jack, Lily, who is older, looks back with enormous affection and remembers him as a real person because he was at home. What would she remember about him if he had just been on a ward, seen a couple of times a week? No, home care is by far the best solution, and I don't understand why, across the board, the HSE system still doesn't openly acknowledge how important it is to get these babies home, not to mention how much money it would save.

Another thing that pushed me towards home care was a meeting I had in the early days, when I was exploring all options, with someone in the Eastern Health Board. At the time, I was thinking of building a unit in Dublin, then if it went well, another unit in Cork. This official was very clear when he said, 'Well, it's amazing what you want to do, and the amount of money you've raised for it, but we probably won't be in a position to fund the staffing of a children's unit.'

I had a sudden vision of a beautiful building and the doors never being unlocked. So that's what really pushed me into home care, which is comparatively inexpensive, and a far warmer, more intimate option for parents. We did a survey some years ago, and 73 per cent of our parents said they would wish, if their child has to die, that they should do so at home, surrounded by familiar things and people who love them.

And yes, I know that it is a desperate thing for any parent to contemplate the death of their child, but for those of us who have a little Jack, or a little Jill, the spectre of their death is a harsh reality from the very beginning, one that we quickly have to get used to confronting. With Jack and Jill children, the quality of their lives really matters, because often there isn't much longevity.

14

SAMSON FORTUNE

About two years into the setting up of the Jack and Jill Foundation, Molly was born. That was a wonderful time for Mary-Ann and me. Her birth lifted some of the profound sadness that was the legacy of Jack's life. Once she came along, gradually the memories of the tubes and syringes receded a little. My in-laws, Mary-Ann's parents, got hysterical when they heard that she was pregnant again, and I can hardly blame them, although I tried to explain that our two children had not died from genetic conditions but through hospital error. Even so, the pregnancy was a terribly anxious time for all of us. Mary-Ann decided to go back to Mount Carmel, where Lily had been born and where she had had a very good experience. The only reason she ever moved was because when she was pregnant with the twins she felt she ought to put safety over comfort and go to a teaching hospital because the advice is always that these are safer. And after the twins were born, and with the tragic loss of John, she had stayed with the teaching hospital when she had Jack, because she thought they would be extra vigilant around her due to her previous history.

That, as we know, didn't quite happen, and so while pregnant with Molly, she returned to Mount Carmel and was tremendously relieved to do so. Everything went very well, and Molly brought so much joy to our lives. I was then the father of seven healthy, living children; my four sons with Mikaela, and two girls and a boy with Mary-Ann.

Shortly before Molly was born, I remember saying to Mary-Ann, 'I can understand what has happened – we have suffered two horrible blows, probably due to human error, but if anyone, or indeed the person who writes the script in heaven, ever takes a healthy child away from me, I don't know what I'll do.' Within two years of saying that, Samson Fortune, my darling youngest son from my first marriage, fell off a wall in the Algarve, where he was on holidays having finished his A-levels. He fell about twelve feet, hit his head off a low brick verge, and he was gone, dead, almost instantly.

He was the third of my sons to die in about six years.

Everyone will always say their dead child was extraordinary, and that is exactly as it should be. But even allowing for that, Sam really was a beautiful boy. So affectionate, so handsome, so brilliant. One of the best ideas I have ever come across came from Sam, who suggested we try to relocate Wimbledon FC to Dublin. I have described the idea in some detail in Chapter 9, and I still think it was a genuinely brilliant scheme. That Sam was just nine when he came up with this, to me shows what a bright and original mind he had.

Sam hadn't gone to Eton like the other boys, because his older brothers and Mikaela didn't like the housemaster he had drawn, so instead he went to a school called Bryanston. I always joked that Mikaela had managed to find the only public school in the UK more expensive than Eton, but it was a very good school and he was very happy there. Mikaela, always a devoted mother, sold her house in London and moved to Dorset to be near him; a year later, he was dead.

It happened during a weekend in August. Sam had finished his A-levels and gone to the Algarve with a group of friends to celebrate. The accident happened during the daytime, there was no alcohol or foolish behaviour involved, just a shocking, terrible, stupid twist of fate. I was in Ireland; Mikaela, who is like a tigress with her cubs, was in England. When the news broke here, it travelled fast. By ten o'clock in the morning, my kitchen was full, with friends and neighbours come to see if they could help in any way. They had brought food, baked cakes, made endless cups of tea and coffee. I like that Irish thing so much. The English don't do it; they hold back, reluctant to intrude on grief. But my experience of grief is that one badly wants to be intruded on. I always think, if I have to go through bad days I would like them to be in Ireland.

Somehow, I had to get to Portugal at short notice on a Sunday in August. Not the easiest thing. But then a most extraordinary thing happened. Denis O'Brien rang me and said, 'I'm so sorry to hear your news. My plane will be available to you at 4 p.m. this afternoon in Dublin airport.' I knew Denis from my days with the Sports Council, and before that I knew his father from my time at Goffs. I thanked him, and said I wanted to pick up one of Sam's brothers, Luke, who was in Southampton. Denis simply said, 'You must just use the plane exactly as you like.' His generosity and decency were extraordinary. So I went and picked up Luke, who is now a very successful rug designer, married to Alice Elliot, niece of Camilla, Duchess of Cornwall. Back then he was a young man, working for Sotheby's, but has always been remarkably level-headed and was a wonderful source of support on that terrible trip.

We got to the Algarve and another very good friend of ours, Rose Fitzjohn, came down to join us. Denis gave me his house for as long as we needed it, and access to his office and staff, to try to get through the awful, awful paperwork and bureaucracy that needed to be dealt with before I could even see my son's body. I'm afraid to say I found Portugal backwards and impossible to navigate administratively. I remember when Madeleine McCann disappeared, I said at the time, 'Those poor people, that is a country that will never solve it.'

Every day seemed to be a bank holiday in Portugal, no one was willing to do anything or help us in any way. We encountered indifference, resistance and callousness, as if we were making a nuisance of ourselves, instead of simply being a family flattened by grief, trying to jump through the necessary hoops so that we could begin the next stage of our dreadful journey. We were told nothing, offices closed without notice and forms were requested without warning. Thanks entirely to Denis O'Brien's office and his wonderful, patient staff, we somehow managed to get through it. Finally, after about a week, I was given a card that allowed me to get the post mortem results (they had found no traces of alcohol or drugs, which just underlined the senselessness of this hideous accident), get an undertaker and pick up Sam's body from the mortuary in Faro. It was something no parent ever wants to do, and I still do not know how I came through it.

Arriving at the mortuary, I felt as though I had stepped straight onto the canvas of a Gustave Doré painting. This was a scene from hell. Gangs of porters stood idly around, hoping for a quick handout, while around them lay corpses on gurneys. I almost had to bid to get my son's body back from these men. They were like the old Dublin 'lockhards': unbearably cruel in their indifference and boredom. That was probably the most distressing moment of my entire life, and if I hadn't had Luke with me, I think I would have lost my reason completely. Eventually we collected our lovely boy and began the process of getting him back on British Airways. Again, I was saved by Denis' office, who took charge of all the necessary administrative matters. The whole thing took forever. We were there for a week at least, constantly trying to get out, get home. Meanwhile, Mikaela couldn't understand why everything was taking so long and was naturally in a terrible state, being comforted by the other two boys, Pirate and Jago, and many friends and relations.

Finally, we were able to get on our way, and I still remember the bleakness of sitting in the departure lounge at Faro with Luke and Rose, surrounded by tourists from UK charter flights on their way home from a sun holiday, chattering, laughing, drinking, comparing tattoos and going heedlessly about their lives, while our extraordinary Sam was gone. It made no sense to me then, and it makes no sense now.

We travelled with Sam's body to Dorset, England, where he was to be buried. On the morning of the funeral, a stunningly bright, sunny day, we came round a corner in the car on our way to the church, and there in front of us, drawn up on common land, was a host of old-fashioned gypsy caravans, painted in bright colours, with huge wooden wheels, smoke coming out of the little chimneys and curtains fluttering in the breeze. It was like the most wonderful Munnings painting, like something from a hundred years ago, and something that Sam would have loved.

Inside, the church was full of Sam's friends, who had come from the four corners of the world. After their A-levels, all these young men and women had scattered far and wide on their gap years, but somehow the news had travelled and they had come back to pay their final respects to their classmate and friend. Mary-Ann and the children were with me, and Phonsie, who was about six at the time, looked so like Sam they could have been twins. There was a discernible ripple through the church when he walked in, people nudging each other and saying, 'He could be a mini Sam.'

Sam is buried close to where Mikaela lives, and I try to get to his grave every time I go to England. I really have no clue how I got through that third terrible tragedy. I know I am very lucky with the people around me, who helped me through. Mikaela was very strong, and I felt I needed to be strong for her too. The children were all wonderful in their own ways, the older ones by being helpful and considerate and kind, the little ones by simply being themselves, with the magic ability that little children have to take you out of yourself and shine a candle on dark moments. Being born with a very phlegmatic temperament also helps. I'm not the type of person – never have been – to indulge in breast-beating and 'Why me?' rants. I tend to just quietly try to get on with things, do what needs to be done, one thing at a time, until enough time passes to allow some healing, and that is what I did.

Of course, being father to six living children also helps. At the time of writing, my eldest son, Pirate, is a journalist with Agence France-Presse in Paris, Luke has his own very successful bespoke rug company, Luke Irwin, with a shop in Pimlico Green, and Jago is a very successful publishing agent and a voting member of BAFTA. Lily is at Exeter University, Phonsie is at UCD, and Molly is passionate about her ponies and represented Ireland twice in 2013 at show jumping.

I don't think it is healthy to allow time to stand still, or to flow past you. I remember when Jack died, at first Mary-Ann was inclined to make a kind of shrine out of his bedroom, to leave it exactly as it had been. I didn't think it was a good idea and after a short while neither did she. Life moves on and that is as it should be. I do remember Mary-Ann saying to me, shortly after Sam died, 'I can't believe we're this bad that we deserve to lose three children.' Certainly, it is very unusual for anyone to lose three sons in peacetime. To see small coffins, to bury your children and have them go into the night before you, is against nature. It was very nearly more than I could bear, but somehow, I have found the strength to go forward from those deaths, and to keep alive the hope of doing some good in the world, with a twinkle in my eye.

15

THE GIFT OF TIME

The motto of the Jack and Jill Foundation is 'The Gift of Time,' by which we mean time free of stress and strain, in which parents can care for their severely ill child, who may not have many years to live, and try to come to terms with what has happened in their family, at their own pace. Time in the healing environment of their own home to understand the needs of their child, and time to develop a bond with him or her, just as they would with any other baby.

That gift of time is only possible through a rigorously worked-out system, however. When we laid down the Foundation documents in 1998, our key objectives with Jack and Jill were:

1. Provide an information brochure to all maternity units in the Republic of Ireland explaining the services offered by the Jack and Jill Foundation.

2. To campaign and lobby to ensure the government recognises and fulfils its obligations to damaged children of four years and under. A campaign should be mounted with the aim of these

children receiving the same rights and entitlements as other members of society with special needs within the time frame of this business plan.

3. To finance homecare charges borne by parents of children with significant disabilities well above and beyond that of the average child up until four years of age.

4. To provide funds to establish a respite unit within a recognised centre.

When I look back at those unsophisticated documents – no fancy spreadsheets or number-crunching tools – I am amazed at the simplicity of our mission and how little it has changed. Some of these objectives have been fully met. Others changed as we discovered more about what was required, and one – namely objective 2 – is an on-going struggle and something that I will come back to in more detail later.

Providing an information brochure to the maternity hospitals was our key bid to try to get the word out that we existed and could help. But it wasn't as easy as you might think to let people know what we were doing. The fact that the health service didn't have any records of children with severe disabilities really didn't help, but actually, there was a lot of resistance initially from the hospitals. I think they thought we were secretly a cover group looking for information in order to possibly sue them for negligence: a front, maybe, for a solicitor's company. So initially anyway, they wouldn't help us to get the message out or refer anybody to us. That did change, over time, though. We went in to all the paediatric hospitals and presented a portfolio of what the Jack and Jill Foundation would do, and asked that if they had any babies that fit the criteria, would they please refer them on. And that's how it started. Once the message got out from parents and families that Jack and Jill had helped them, things began to gather momentum. As the hospitals heard back from families we had helped about what we actually did, they were delighted to have something to recommend to parents in these sad situations.

We also distributed brochures in doctors' surgeries through-out the country and I jumped at every chance I got to speak on radio. Our first children came about through word of mouth – somebody knew somebody, who knew Mary-Ann and me, or who was based geographically close to where we lived and had heard about Jack. Bit by bit, the word started to travel. Initially, we even encountered some reluctance from parents themselves, particularly those parents whose children hadn't been born with a serious condition, but who had developed this later, through illness or accident. It was very difficult for them to admit that their child had become in need of so much medical assistance, was probably never going to improve very much, and was now a Jack and Jill child. Many held out for a surprisingly long time before realising that they simply couldn't continue without support.

Nobody ever expects Jack or Jill to happen in their lives. If the signs of brain damage are there at birth, the hospital will tell you straightaway, but it could well be not until the six-week check-up that a problem is identified. Or the public health nurse might spot that something isn't right. A lot of Jack and Jill cases are genetic but some are the result of mistakes in hospital, usually at the time of birth. Some are the result of illness, such as meningitis, others seem to happen around the time of childhood vaccinations, although no link has yet been established. These tragedies don't just happen to one section of society, they happen from Aylesbury Road and Montenotte, through to council flats and suburban estates. Our constituents are a kaleidoscope of society, single girls with drug problems and HIV in the inner city of Dublin; affluent middle-class, educated women; and everyone in between. All are equally as likely to have a little Jack or a Jill, which means that we have the whole rainbow of society to observe.

It also means our nurses need to be able to meet and deal with every type of person. In each case we have to make sure that the nurse gets on with the mother in particular. Sometimes, mothers are so highly strung, so close to the end of their tether, so flattened by the strain of their circumstances, that you need to just be there for them. They are so frustrated, having been battling so hard, filling out endless forms and answering endless questions. Meanwhile their babies are probably screaming all the time; they might have other children and be feeling guilty because they aren't spending time with them, trying to juggle everything. Some of our mothers are very close to going into hospital themselves. Into that chaos, our nurses bring calm, a sense of order and possibility, a shoulder to put to the common wheel. They are all wonderful, warm and competent women, able to fill the role of friend and confidante as much as nurse.

Often they become so close to these families that they are like an aunt or a best friend. From that position they see, and often assist with, the emotional fall-out of a Jack or Jill child, as much as with medical matters.

Exactly as the paediatrician explained to Mary-Ann and me after Jack was born, there is a very real danger of partnerships and marriages splitting up once a little Jack or Jill enters the family. I don't know why, but blame comes out onto the table, even though these things are never the fault of the families. Personally, I think the fundamental problem with an awful situation such as a child with disabilities, is that all too often the male gender can react very differently and, perhaps because they don't know what to do instinctively, can appear to be doing nothing. A mother's instinct is to grab that baby, no matter how bleak the prognosis, and hold on to it. In our experience men feel helpless, redundant, even pushed away. And they don't get much help with that. In hospital, after Jack had his terrible seizure, I remember that Mary-Ann got counselled out of her tree, whereas no one ever came near me. Now, I rather like healing myself, rather than having someone else try to do it, but I was surprised that nothing was offered to me, or even to the two of us jointly. This may help explain why dads sometimes handle these situations so badly.

Over the years, I've noticed that even if the marriage partnership is good, dad probably works a bit more, plays a bit more golf, basically goes into denial around what has happened, while mum holds the fort at home. But where the partnership isn't that strong to start with, a Jack or Jill child will often deliver the final blow, and we have seen many relationships simply break under the pressure. The dad walks, which means mum is then left even more alone, often with other young children to look after. Where we get into real trouble is where the parents are very young – seventeen, eighteen, nineteen years old, and not married. In those cases, daddy is usually gone the next day and often not heard from again.

The strain of a Jack or Jill child is very serious. The first shock is emotional, of course, but on the heels of emotional trauma comes finances – the sheer cost of having a child who is brain-damaged – quickly joined by the social isolation. Our mothers mostly have to give up work, if they have been working, and so they immediately lose the social ambiance that goes with employment. Their baby takes up so much time, simply to feed and care for, that they find it incredibly difficult to get out of the house, and friends often don't wish to call over because they are afraid they will be in the way, that mum is too busy, or that they will say something stupid. So the loneliness is horrible. These babies are even more overwhelming than, say, a grave financial problem, because they are relentless, poor little things, and there is no real hope of their recovering. You can always daydream about winning the lottery to sort out financial worries, but there is no medical equivalent for a badly damaged child. With these babies, there are no miracles. I don't want to try to stop people going to salt mines in Romania, or to New York for advanced brain techniques, or whatever else they have pinned their faith on, but in our experience there never are miracles. I remember when Jack was born, there were a couple of lovely old ladies who used to come in with a relic of Padre Pio and spend half an hour with Jack, praying. I will say that he was often calmer afterwards, but he was never going to suddenly leap up like Lazarus.

I do think we have saved a lot of partnerships over the years, simply by placing someone else there, within the family, who is professional and able and calm, and by taking a lot of the financial burden of nursing these children. I would never be so bold as to claim credit for those partnerships that survive, but I do think we have helped. Unlike the HSE, which is so full of rules and regulations, we are able to work very closely with our families, tailor what we do to what they need and not put up resistance to them: after all, we're doing this for them, and we are mindful that every family is different.

From the very start, 60 per cent of my time was spent not on administration or fund-raising matters, but on simply being an advocate for my families, so that their child actually gets what the state should, in my view, automatically be giving them. By 'being an advocate', I sometimes mean just sitting it out on the end of the phone as our very reasonable requests – a few hours of respite care, housing grants, conversion grants, delivery of equipment – were passed around from pillar to post and back again, with long periods on hold in between.

The HSE's primary aim seems to be to protect budgets at all costs and never to set precedents. The people our parents were encountering on the end of the phone when they rang to inquire about assistance, support, medical cards – all the things they so badly needed – were so obnoxious, so rude, they were like a brick wall of indifference. Just think about a mother with a tiny baby who needs twenty-four-hour care, possibly with other children as well, maybe even a job, and consider what it means to her to be put on hold again and again, passed around from one department and official to another, never getting a straight answer or even a sympathetic response!

As an example, here is a copy of the standard HSE letter to parents looking for a medical card for a seriously ill child:

I refer to your recent application for a Medical Card/GP Visit Card which is currently on hold.

In order to process your application as quickly as possible, please submit evidence in relation to the items listed below, as soon as possible. Your application will be considered closed unless this additional information is received to support your application within 21 days from the date of this letter.

Item/s Required:

Evidence of fire and contents insurance i.e. letter from insurance provider detailing repayment amount and frequency or recent bank statement (where account holder's name is visible) showing instances of insurance payment being made.

Evidence of mortgage payments i.e. recent mortgage account statement showing deductions made or recent bank statement showing instances of mortgage payments being made where the name of the mortgage provider is shown clearly.

Evidence of your expenses incurred in respect of childcare costs i.e. letter from childcare facility detailing weekly/monthly cost.

Evidence of your expenses incurred in travel to work e.g. copy of Vehicle Registration Certificate, public transport ticket etc. Please confirm location of employment and weekly distance travelled, if not already detailed on the application.

Evidence of your mortgage protection payments i.e. letter from protection provider detailing repayment amount and frequency or recent bank statement (where account holder's name is visible) showing instances of protection payment being made.

Evidence of your savings and investments i.e. statement from each financial institution in which an account is held showing details of current savings/investments. Share Certificates showing shareholdings, rather than dividends received should be submitted.

Evidence of your spouse/partner's employment/self employment i.e. latest Notice of Assessment from the Revenue Commissioners, or Revenue Commissioners letter of non-liability for tax. If the business has ceased trading please submit relevant letter from Revenue Commissioners.

Evidence of your spouse/partner's expenses incurred in travel to work e.g. Copy of Vehicle Registration Certificate, public transport ticket etc. Please confirm location of employment and weekly distance travelled, if not already detailed on the application.

Evidence of your spouse/partner's wages i.e. recent payslip or most recent P45 if employment has ceased.

Evidence of your wages i.e. recent payslip or most recent P45 if employment has ceased.

All this within twenty-one days – not even twenty-one working days – or your case is closed. At a time when fate has just dealt you probably the greatest blow of your life. And by the time the letter arrives, it has taken two days to get to you, meaning the clock is already ticking, fast. Nowhere is there any mention of your child or a single expression of sympathy. Even if that expression of compassion were a formality, nothing more than a conventional one-line acknowledgement, it would be decent to include it. Why should any scrap of humanity be deemed so incompatible with efficiency?

It was as if the government calculated that if they fobbed off these exhausted, traumatised parents enough, they would just give up. Reasonable requests were dealt with by people so deeply unsympathetic, who seemed to be going out of their way to block access to help and support, that, before we came along, many of these parents did give up. They stopped asking for help, because they couldn't cope any more with the indifferent response.

However, Mary Joe Guilfoyle and I had plenty of time and energy to fight these battles, and we were determined to do that. In the early days, before we were really set up to offer much more than money and moral support, this was something we could and did do. We were prepared to stay on hold for as long as it took to answer the same questions put by five different people, to explain our case again and again, to keep our tempers and our emotions in check and persist until we got the help needed for our families. That may sound like a small thing – being able to sit it out on hold, be passed through departments, answer questions put in a dry and unsympathetic manner – but actually, to these beleaguered parents, it was a huge deal.

We have carried on doing this. Our nurse-managers are extraordinary – there are twelve of them, all very different, highly qualified, very warm paediatric nurses. The way the Jack and Jill Foundation works is that we have over 600 registered nurses on a database. These are not employees of the Jack and Jill Foundation. They are co-ordinated by the nurse-managers, who are our full-time employees. Whatever the cost of the care that we have agreed with a particular family, a parent (usually mum) sends us a charge sheet at the end of each month and we send them a cheque to cover the cost as a donation from Jack and Jill. From that they pay their nurse, so the nurses are actually employed by the families. We are a charity, not a nursing agency. Meanwhile the nurse-managers make sure the right nurse goes into each situation – there is no point having someone mum doesn't get on with – and take on the burden of dealing with the HSE and other bureaucratic matters. They are supported by six full-time and five part-time staff members in the office: in contrast to many of the bigger charities, who might have a minimum of ten people in the fund-raising department alone.

A lot of their work is picking up the first alarm bells of families who simply aren't getting the care they need, even now.

For example, someone who is living in appalling conditions and isn't being rehoused, who isn't getting a grant to adapt their car to carry a child like Jack, who might need very particular equipment and special adjustments that are very expensive (for example, they might need a bath adapted as a child grows older and heavier). They take those battles on and usually will sort those problems out. But every now and again one of them will ring me and say, 'This is really a nightmare.' And then I come rolling into action.

I don't have a temper, but I have a sense of injustice for other people, and I have no problem being very forthright with an officer in the HSE, no matter how smart his or her title. I will write to them, explaining the situation, asking them to ring me back by return. And I will probably go the traditional Irish route too and write to the family's local TDs. I don't think we've ever been thwarted once we set our mind to something, whereas the parents themselves are so exhausted, so traumatised, that they are unable to keep going, keep fighting for what should be theirs by right.

When we started the Jack and Jill Foundation, there wasn't a satisfactory health care package for these families at all. The world that Mary Joe and I stepped into was really bleak. Happily, that has improved, and the HSE is beginning to see that rather than bringing the child back into hospital all the time, care in the community works – largely thanks to us, I think. We have children aged ten, twelve and fourteen who were initially given two months to live, and yet they have flourished in their own homes, surrounded by love, care and warmth. The HSE has now instituted outreach nurses, which is a big step, but some of the nurses they are providing come from nursing agencies and still don't have the right training; for example they don't know how to cope with a tracheotomy. And they stop work at 4 p.m. on a Friday. We leave here when our job is done, and not before. We don't go anywhere until everything is finished for the day and the week. The physical circumstances of what the HSE provides have improved somewhat, but the attitude hasn't.

If you are a parent of a little Jack and Jill child, from the day our liaison nurse walks into your life, your life changes and your sense of panic goes away. Our team will be on the doorstep by the time you get back from hospital; I could get a referral today and we would have a nurse there tonight. And that nurse is like part of the family, always there, always at the end of the phone. They don't work weekends, but if they need to get up in the middle of the night on a Saturday night because they have a palliative baby in their care who suddenly needs them, they will do it. Their commitment is 24/7 and there is no overtime; they do it because they love these babies.

We try to help the families as a whole, rather than just the child, because we know how important it is to try to maintain some semblance of normality for the siblings, to give parents some time off and time away, and give our children as much joy and peace in their lives as we can manage. Each year we organise a family day at Kilmainham. This started roughly ten years ago because we realised how isolated our families were. So once a year, they all come to Kilmainham for a spectacular day. The army, the mounted police, the fire brigade, the Garda

Band, all donate their time for free. We get them to come just by asking. They all know about Jack and Jill, and if they can, they want to help. We have armoured cars on display, snipers hidden in the ground that the children have to try to spot. This drives the little boys wild with excitement, and I know some people will say, 'Oh, you shouldn't encourage them to have an interest in guns and tanks,' but I feel that you can't stop them. The thrill for those children of being so close to mounted police, soldiers and so on, is huge.

It is a truly wonderful day, with past and present families there. Many of the families don't want to wean themselves off, even after their child has passed away. They have become so attached to being part of this club that they like to come back. And it is a way of remembering their son or daughter with other people who knew him or her, and who understand some of their pain. It should be a very sad club, but as our new chairman, David Reid-Scott, said last year when he came for the first time – 'Where are the tears?' In fact it is a joyful day, where children play, dads lose some of their wicked shyness, mums can talk to other mums, people who know what the daily struggles of their lives are. We provide reflexology for stressed parents and a sensory room for our special needs children that is darkened, with projectors on the ceiling and fibre optic lights; food, drink, a sense of fun.

We do other odd things. Nestlé recently gave us 300 tickets for all our families to one of the cinemas in Dundrum for a morning showing of a children's film, along with wonderful goodie bags. That was a surprise for them: they could go along

THE GIFT OF TIME

with all their children, give them a day out. And then the siblings start to think, 'We got this because of little Jack or little Jill,' so instead of resentment around a child that is taking up so much parental time and attention, there is a feeling of gratitude. Towards the end of last year, Zurich Insurance held a week-long international conference in Dublin, and, as Zurich Ireland have chosen us as their particular charity, I was asked to speak at the conference. Afterwards, at each table were ten really superior teddy bears and ten boxes of clothes, and all the managers and their wives were asked to dress the teddy bears, put them into a fancy box, with the name of one of our children on the box. These were delivered to all our children in the run-up to Christmas, as a complete surprise. We try to do these things outside of donating the monthly cheque, in order to make our families feel that they are regarded and cared about, that they are people in their own right, not just numbers on a HSE database.

We send birthday cards to all our children; sometimes we get twins, and one is healthy and the other is a Jack and Jill child, but we always send cards to both. The challenge is to scale up the work of the Foundation, but still keep the humanity and the homeliness. So many charities, once they get big, just become vast bureaucracies, more worried about Croke Park or Haddington Road than anything else. Our priority has always been the children and their families. We are here to fight their battles, ease their path, work with them and cheer for them.

16

THE BIG BATTLES

Since starting the Jack and Jill Foundation in 1997, I have been awarded Irish Fundraiser of the Year (2011), Global Fundraiser of the Year (2011), and recently Chevalier of St Lazare and Honorary Fellow of the Faculty of Paediatrics. The Foundation has been awarded Charity of the Year (2003), raised nearly €50 million for the care of brain-damaged children and become something very close to a household name in this country. We have fought countless battles, publicly and privately on behalf of the most vulnerable citizens of the state, and won the majority of these. And yet, flattering as it is to get awards, when I look back at the key objectives of the Jack and Jill Foundation, as laid out by Wendy and myself in our policy documents in 1997, the second item on the list still stands out, for all the wrong reasons:

> To campaign and lobby to ensure the government recognises and fulfils its obligations to damaged children of four years and under. A campaign should be mounted with the aim of these children receiving the same rights and entitlements as other members of society with special needs within the time frame of this Business Plan.

Tragically, after sixteen years and despite constant effort on our part, that hasn't happened as fully as I had hoped. To be fair, a bit of light has come through, and the situation now for babies with major disabilities is better than it was, but it still isn't good enough. Government behaviour towards these children remains in large part very shocking. Over the years, we have been to so many meetings and Oireachtas hearings, and my experience is that the politicians don't know what's really happening – because the HSE is not open enough.

The 2013 controversy over the withdrawal of medical cards is a typical example. Politicians were standing up in the Dáil and insisting that nothing to do with the issue of medical cards had changed, whereas in fact everything had changed. In the end the government had to do an embarrassing u-turn, when it became apparent how unpopular their reforms were with everyone, not just medical card holders. The cards they had confiscated were reinstated.

The Children's Referendum of 2012 cost almost €13 million, yet nothing tangible has improved. Children are still being overlooked and ignored. At no stage, for example, has the government ever stepped forward and asked us, 'What can we do to help?' Even now, their primary aim seems to be to protect budgets.

The government still doesn't have a paediatric homecare budget, which means that we still regularly hear about children trapped in hospital, sometimes for years, because they can't go home. And they can't go home because there is no system or budget to care for them, which means they lead their entire lives within the confines of the hospital, like something out of the Victorian era, and their families are subject to immense strain as a result. This, apart from being cruel and unnecessary, is very costly. A child nursed at home by the Jack and Jill Foundation will cost €16,000 a year. If the same child is left in hospital, that cost will be €150,000. The money being spent is tax-payer money – our money – and still the government will not commit to making that saving. There are various reasons for this, one being that no part of the hospital budget can be put into the homecare budget; they must be kept completely separate. The system is like a bockety old ladder tied together with bits of string.

The HSE is one of the richest health agencies in the world, yet it has outsourced a lot of what it should be doing itself, in a modern, First World country such as Ireland, to charities. The government hands over vast sums – around €4 billion a year – to do various jobs, such as caring for the homeless, the old, the poor, that it should be doing itself. And it has no idea how this money is being spent. There are no figures for what goes where and what the money is used for. This is appalling.

Quite apart from the fact that this, in and of itself, is quite clearly wrong, there is then a real problem with degrees of separation. At what point does a charity become an arm of government? When it is 50 per cent state-funded? 70 per cent? More? Such charities can then no longer speak out about the failures of government: they are hobbled. And they tend to carry very high administrative costs, because they are essentially operating like a government body. Many have reached the stage where they are more worried about salaries, working hours, conditions and the Haddington Road agreement, than the people they are ostensibly caring for.

The Jack and Jill Foundation receives €519,000 of the €2.7 million it needs each year from the HSE. The rest – more than 80 per cent of its funding – comes from the public. That money funds intensive home nursing care for children with life-limiting conditions, from birth to four years old, as well as end-of-life care for children who are sent home to die. We have to raise this money ourselves, simply to stay afloat. We have to innovate, invent and stay constantly on top of new ideas, and this keeps us working hard and smart, unlike so many charities funded up to 70 per cent by the government. And our money is working hard for us. I know some charities like to keep huge reserves in the bank – millions, sometimes – but we don't believe in doing that. Ideally, we would like to have the equivalent of three years' funds safely stored in case of a financial monsoon, but I don't want money that has been generously donated to care for sick children sitting in some bank vault.

The HSE grant covers the cost of our fund-raising division in terms of accounts, HR, IT and the fund-raising team, including my salary, which means that money donated by the public goes directly to fund home nursing for children. My salary is just under €90,000 today, something that I have always been very open about. I am well paid and I'm not shy about that; any charity CEO who won't answer questions about their salary is, in my mind, behaving in a way that lacks credibility. There are no top-ups, bonuses or pension payments added to my salary, in any shape or form. For the first six years of running Jack and Jill, I didn't take a salary, although I was working seven days a week. Even now, this is still a seven-day-a-week role, and even though I have a fancy title – CEO – in reality I am all things within the team; I order the stationery, buy the loo paper, answer the phones, take donations, whatever is needed at a particular time on any particular day.

In my own mind, I can justify taking a salary on the basis that since we began in 1997 we have supported 1,700 children with home nursing care and raised nearly €50 million privately, thanks to the generosity of the Irish people. During that time we have received just €4.5 million from the health service. So as a percentage of the fund-raising I've done, my salary works out at less than 2 per cent.

We are living on our wits already, yet the government has steadily chipped away at those funds it does give us. Not only are they cutting us at source, cuts of a couple of per cent every year across the board, but they are also leaving more and more children to live off our funds rather than their funds. Before, we would have shared nursing hours with them. Now they say, 'We have no money,' and so we are picking up the slack. Because we cannot let a family drop into the void, not when we know what that void is, our budgets are having to stretch ever further.

We save the HSE a fortune every year but they don't seem to like us one bit. We identified a great niche in the market – a niche of terror and horror and indignity, yes – but we did identify it and have filled it, and in doing so have shown up the

HSE's deficiencies in a big way. We have proved that there is nothing impossible about caring for very sick children and their families, that it can be done – humanely and cost-effectively – and therefore asked the question: why was the HSE not doing it? Why is the HSE still not doing it?

When I started the Jack and Jill Foundation, I never thought I would still be running the charity sixteen years later. My ideal, frankly, was that Jack and Jill would light the way, and then withdraw gracefully. Some time ago we thought the time had come: 'Right, we've shown them what to do, and what needs to be done, so let's hand the reins over to the health service, where they belong.' So in 1999 or 2000, we did a small vox pop, through our nurses, of parents, asking them how they would feel if Jack and Jill was dismantled and our work absorbed by the health service. The reaction of these families was one of absolute horror. They went barmy. They felt as if they were being thrown to the wolves – rather slothful wolves, but wolves nonetheless – and that the whole system that we had set up and that works so well, would be a shambles within six months. And so we didn't do it, couldn't abandon them, and here we are still. Somehow, without signposts, we seem to have turned onto the right road every time.

Of the 300-odd babies in our care at any one time, I estimate that at least 120 would go straight back into hospital if the Jack and Jill Foundation were to disband, with the resulting cost to government, which is quite obviously very ill at ease with paediatric care for the under-fours. They don't appear on the radar. Go to any healthcare conference and it is as if these children simply don't exist. They are not discussed, nor are their needs recognised. In fact, I think that such are their failures in this field, that rather than us disband, I sometimes think the government should withdraw entirely, and that rather than trying to organise a patchwork quilt of care, they should leave the work to those who understand and care about it. They don't have a paediatric homecare budget, and even though the staff at ground level are mostly very good and highly-regarded by my own team, problems arise because of the overwhelming wait times and administration required.

All our nurses are empowered in their own right to walk into a house to say, 'Yes, this is a Jack and Jill child,' and set the wheels of assistance in motion. Later, the nurse will tell me the basis for her decision and I am in a position to move things forward immediately. In addition, our nurses are mistresses of their own time; they are not filling out endless paperwork – we take charge of that in the office for them – they have arms around the child and their family from the start. Meanwhile, a nurse from the HSE team will make the same assessment, but she has to send for approval upstream, and we have known babies to die in the time it takes for that approval to come though and for help to be given.

How many times does that have to happen before people lose all initiative? The greatest criticism of the HSE is coming from their staff on the ground. There is great disquiet about the number of offices empty in these vast glass palaces that are still being heated and lit twenty-four hours a day. It is very dispiriting to be working for such an organisation. From our perspective, the HSE has grown into a gigantic whale, so gigantic that reforms look to be almost impossible. I would love there to be reform, but I don't see how that is possible, so forceful are the powers of negativity.

We generally have very good relationships with the HSE at a local level, but once you start climbing the ladder and coming up against longer and longer titles, the people apparently become more and more unable to act. And at that level, they are virtually impossible to meet. They seem to have endless meetings with each other, but seldom with anyone 'on the ground'. The senior management of the HSE do not appear to want or, possibly, to be able to accept any initiatives from the outside. Under these circumstances our families can be nothing more than numbers on a computer screen to them, not real people with real life-changing problems.

And so there are still considerable challenges ahead of us. Right now, one of my biggest battles is the question of medical cards for our Jack and Jill children, and this is one that won't seem to go away. I have never been able to understand why the children are not assessed in their own right, and why the government insists that the parents have to be means tested. I don't believe there is another section of society where a third party has to intervene like this. The last two United Nations reports into childcare in Ireland both insisted that children with medical needs should receive a card in their own right, without any means testing of parents. And it is so very easy to fail the means test: even though the margins have been broadened slightly in recent years, it is not enough. A family on a perfectly average, medium-to-low income will usually fail, even though you need the wealth of the Aga Khan to adequately care for a child with profound disabilities.

Frankly, I don't care how well off you are – if a baby like Jack enters your life, that child should still be given a medical card. And that is something that the HSE and government just don't seem to understand. I remember a health official said to me in honest bafflement, 'But surely all children need the same things – a cot, a few bottles, a buggy.' My response was, 'Come and spend a day in one of our houses and see the kind of requirements these children have, for equipment that, without which, their already difficult lives will be even more appalling.' Every year we get a form from the HSE, with about twenty-two blank pages, asking for details of any complaints received about us during the year. To which I respond – and small wonder – 'The only complaints we have ever received are about yourselves.'

These poor parents would do anything for their child, yet the first time they try to engage with Official Ireland and get something of real value to their child, a medical card, they fail the means test, which makes them feel they have failed their darling child again. What they do sometimes get is a temporary medical card – usually valid for about six months, which means that every six months they have to jump through all the hoops again. And these cards are often withdrawn for the most extraordinary reasons, ones that make no sense: your child is no better, is often worse and the card may be summarily taken away.

In an ideal world, all children who qualify for Jack and Jill status would automatically qualify for a medical card. That was in fact suggested by Brian Lenihan when he was Minister of State for Health, but the civil servants poo-pooed it. In fact, in my experience, the ministers usually understand – especially Mary Harney, when she was Minister for Health – but there is simply no way of pushing change through the organisation. And because 300 children a year dotted around the country doesn't amount to a voice in any one constituency, these families are deemed unimportant politically, so no one will go to bat for them.

Another major challenge is succession. Who takes over from me? How do we create the follow-on? It's a funny job, this one. You can't just do it as a suit. I believe you need a parent, a Jack and Jill parent, with experience of fund-raising, rather than just a CEO sitting behind a desk. You need somebody with a passion, who understands the lives these families are catapulted into when a little Jack or Jill is born. Somebody who has been in the valley and knows the view from down there. I'm not trained to do anything really, but I can speak to these parents, because we're speaking as equals. I can say to them, 'I know what you are going through.'

I remember when Jack died, it was just so sad. He was never going to have quality of life, but those little babies take a part of your heart you can't believe. After the first appalling wave of grief, I confess that we actually settled into a slight sense of relief. Mostly for him – there were no more plugs in his arm, no more tubes up his nose, no more fits, no more pain. But then, I have to say, relief for Family Irwin. The brother and sister could get their lives back, we could suddenly lead a normal life again. Now, feeling a sense of relief when your child has just died seems very unnatural, but actually, in those circumstances, it isn't. What I have managed to do at the bereavement meetings that I've chaired is tell parents it's all right to feel some kind of relief. There are usually a dozen parents there – and the thing I will say is just that. 'You must not be feeling guilty because somewhere inside you is a feeling of relief … it is a perfectly natural reaction.' Nobody ever talks to them about that sort of thing. I am not a trained counsellor, or anything of the sort, but if you've been through something like that, you can talk about it.

As for what comes next for Jack and Jill, I do not see any great changes to our Foundation. What we do works perfectly. We run a very tight budget and in ten years I imagine we will be doing largely the same thing. Medical advancements will continue and it is likely that we will end up with fewer children with fewer health issues. But alas there will always be medical negligence; there will always be healthy children who get meningitis or suffer physical trauma that leaves them damaged. There will always be Jack and Jill babies. I don't think there are any miracles waiting in the wings. There is work being done on stimulating brain cells to try and reverse the process of brain damage, but this is still in its relative infancy, and there will always be children who cannot be helped by this.

Yet another significant challenge has come through my own health recently. Which is terribly annoying. Illness is not a question of fate. You don't get cancer because it's your fate to get cancer, it's just another nightmare of life, far too prevalent, and something that paid me a visit recently.

I've always had wonderful health, and so I never think about it. So when, just over a year ago, I suddenly had the most terrifying haemorrhage – blood everywhere, so that I looked as if I was in an abattoir, I refused to take it seriously and just thought, 'Oh, its piles or something.' I mean, I don't even know how my body works, so even though I nearly died of terror, I presumed this nightmare would just go away, and it did. Nothing else happened for about six weeks, at which stage I had almost forgotten my fright and was congratulating myself on not hysterically rushing off to the doctor, when it suddenly happened for a second time.

It was morning time and I was at home – luckily – so I went downstairs, and Mary-Ann noticed immediately that something was wrong. She told me I looked awfully wan and pale, so I had to pluck up my courage and tell her, even though I would far rather have ignored the whole thing. I know that is so pathetic, but that's how men are and I'm the most pathetic of all men. We are terrified of going to be examined. I seriously thought, 'God, I don't need all this hassle,' which is so utterly stupid when the alternative is death.

Luckily, Mary-Ann wasn't prepared to listen to me. She rang our doctor, who said, 'Right, he's to come in here straight away this morning.' In fact, he took one look at me and I was sent off to St Vincent's Private Hospital, about three hours later. By that time I'd lost so much blood they had to give me three bags of it just to stabilise me.

There we were, Mary-Ann, young Phonsie and I, in a room, and the doctor came in and cheerily announced, 'Oh, yes, he's got rectal cancer.' After him came an absolute procession of doctors, I was positively inundated with them, each one nicer than the last. Denis O'Brien very kindly offered to fly me to Sloan Kettering in the States and pay for the treatment, but I found St Vincent's Private Hospital to be world class. I was so impressed by it: built in two years, delivered on budget at €100 million. Meanwhile the government is planning to spend €650 million on the Children's Hospital, with €50 million already spent, and not a brick or girder to show for it. The go-ahead spirit of private enterprise is conspicuously lacking from that project.

I was immediately put on a month's treatment of radiation and mobile chemo, meaning I was discharged with a chemo-therapy bottle in my pocket, a bit like a baby's bottle, with a tube that ran up and into a portal in my chest. It is a bit of a bore, because it can't ever be disconnected, and neither can it get wet, so you're trying to wash your hair with one hand while holding the bottle with the other. However, not so long ago I would have had to stay in hospital for all five weeks, lying there, letting the chemo steadily drip into my system, unable to move about much.

The week after chemo started, I went in for my first session of daily radiotherapy, and then every week for five weeks. Again, it was a bit of a bore, but very efficient and the team were charming. I wouldn't, for preference, have to go in front of four nurses every day and pull my knickers down and have my bottom zapped, but actually, you don't really give a damn after a while. And the nurses did say it was the nicest bottom they'd ever seen!

Through it all I had no side effects, apart from quite a sore bottom. In fact, I was surprised that I felt so well and was so chirpy. It really wasn't a question of being 'extraordinarily brave' – there was very little to be brave about. The nurses were mighty, we had such laughs, and I kept feeding them with Lily O'Brien's chocolates.

Cancer is still a word to bring a shudder of fear to most of us, but by girding our loins and giving the professionals the earliest opportunity to work their wiles, we give them a good chance to save us. If we don't, they can't. You won't bring down the incidence of diagnosis, but if we can bring the mortality rate down, that is already something.

So cancer, which initially seemed such a terrifying diagnosis, in fact turned out to be quite manageable. Four months after my radiation and chemo treatments, I was operated on, and that was very successful. Sadly, there has been a knock-on from the four hours I spent on the operating table. My treatment was hugely successful at eradicating the cancer and I am entirely clear of it. However, the surgery has left me with quite a different problem. I now have something called a dropped foot, which is very painful and debilitating, and means I cannot use my foot or ankle at all. This is not uncommon following a major operation, although it took quite some time for it to be acknowledged and it was evident from the morning after the operation that my foot was dragging. Since then it has got worse and worse so that now I am unable to put any weight on that leg, and am constantly on crutches or in a wheelchair.

What I find extraordinary is that mainstream medicine simply washes its hands and says there is nothing they can do: 'You'll never walk or drive again in your life,' is roughly what they tell you – not at all what one wants to hear. In my case no one can do anything to help, except kill the pain by using pain blockers in the back. There is apparently no question of resuscitating the nerves or getting traction back into the leg so that I am able to lift my foot or use my ankle. And I am by no means the only person this has happened to.

What stuns me is that I was diagnosed with a terrifying, killer affliction – cancer – that turned out to be OK, but that this has led to a very mundane unattractive thing that is not going to kill me but is destroying my quality of life by leaving me unable to do the simplest things. If I leave anything upstairs or downstairs, I have to ask someone else to get it for me. I have to be driven to every appointment and helped in and out of the car. I am hampered in my visits to my Jack and Jill families, and to the schools where I speak. I can't pop down to the shops for a newspaper or out for a walk. More than ever, I understand some of the restrictions and lack of dignity that are the lot of people with disabilities. It is not a bad perspective for anyone to have, but the gaining of it has been hard indeed.

Meantime, because mainstream medicine has washed its hands of me, I have stepped into the alternative world of complementary medicine, where, because it is unregulated and largely unrecognised, you never know if you are walking into the office of a snake-oil salesman or a gifted healer. So far, there have been no miracles, but I live in hope. And I know that, despite the pain and discomfort and sheer awkwardness of being so crippled, I have no intention of giving up the good fight for better conditions for vulnerable people.

17

POACHER TURNED GAMEKEEPER

At the age of seventy-two, with one bad leg, I have decided I am going to run for office as an Independent in the 2016 general election. This may seem unexpected, but I have always had a strong interest in politics. When I was younger, however, I presumed that with my accent I hadn't a hope of being elected. Now I am so fed up that I don't care about my accent at all any more – largely because I think other people, too, are so fed up that they will see beyond it.

Being discontented is rooted in a kind of grumpy old man syndrome. I cannot believe that the Coalition, who achieved a thumping landslide, should be so lacking in vision and enthusiasm. They came in on such a sweeping majority, with so many young TDs, that I thought we would enter really exciting times. But instead of the change they promised, what has happened? Same old, same old, basically. The elderly are back in control, cronies on state boards, apathy, lack of imagination and ideas. I have always accepted that if you are sufficiently dissatisfied about something, you have to try to effect change yourself. That is the stage at which I now find myself.

I'm clearly not the only one. Polls show that the Don't-Knows are at 33 per cent, which is very high. I believe there is a real wish to get away from the old system of party politics and find a different way. If I am prepared to try to do something about this, with only one good leg and at seventy-three years of age, there must be other younger men and women out there with energy and commitment who can too. My aim in coming out and announcing my candidacy so early is to try to encourage those people, persuade them that there is a point in them stepping forward, in the hope that enough of us might lead to the dawn of something new in politics.

Am I daunted by the kind of energy that will be required to see this through? No, actually, because I am not planning on being the kind of politician who survives by focusing on minuscule local issues. I'm not going to collect your dustbins or tarmac your road. I'll let the county councillors do that, as they should be doing it. My focus will be on national politics, the big picture of life in this country.

The Jack and Jill Foundation runs so smoothly now that my absence will be easily dealt with. In any case, it is time to hand the reins on to someone else, someone with whom I can work closely when needed, but can also allow to do their own thing. At the same time, being elected as a TD would mean that I can move closer to matters within the HSE and effect change from the inside.

I feel comfortable representing the elderly and those with disabilities and would certainly be at the forefront of related issues like the fight for medical cards. I suppose you can say

I come to the polling booths with a slight advantage, namely fifty years of commercial life, since I decided to emigrate to Ireland in 1959, just as many of the brightest and best left this island for opportunities around the globe. In terms of my history in Kildare, I have lived in both the north and south of the county. I brought Goffs there in 1974–5 and cemented Kildare as the centre of the thoroughbred industry. I'm still a member of the Turf Club and very concerned at the fact that the Curragh, which is unique in that it hosts every one of the five classic races of its nation, making it a vital part of the industry, is falling to pieces. Its facilities are simply unacceptable in the twenty-first century. The Turf Club, which owns the racecourse, has no money, and it is very difficult to construct an attractive business plan for potential investors. I find it extraordinary that the agricultural committee in Leinster House hardly ever discusses this industry, which is of international excellence. I think racing has to change its attitude, to become more central to the heartbeat of political Ireland. I also find it extraordinary that the breeders of this country are unique in that they insist on selling their best horses with English sales companies, to the great detriment of Ireland Inc. and the world-class sales companies we have here in Ireland. I feel strongly that the industry cannot demand massive grants from the government, and indeed tax-payers, while at the same time being quite content to stab the Irish sales industry in the back.

Through my role as husband of Mary-Ann O'Brien and director of Lily O'Brien's, job creation is close to my heart and indeed I regard it as a pathway back to prosperity for the nation. Lily O'Brien's currently employs 120 people, rising to 150 at the busiest times of year. This is a company which started in a saucepan twenty-four years ago. Senior politicians consistently bang on about how important entrepreneurs are, yet they allow the Department of Finance and Revenue to make life difficult for those self-same entrepreneurs. At the moment the self-employed seem to be treated by the tax office as pariahs, and until such time as politicians are prepared to lead and reform, entrepreneurs will continue to refuse to come forward and create jobs.

My appeal as a candidate will be to the Don't-Knows and the squeezed middle classes, who feel they are being overlooked and over-taxed. The 20 per cent in any constituency who never vote are an interesting challenge too – they are an uneaten dinner, and I feel that I understand some of their reservations around political engagement. Most people in my social circle have no regard for politics whatsoever because they feel that the people in Dáil Éireann don't represent them. There are too many backbenchers who are emasculated by government whips because of the size of the majority, meaning that all these bright, committed people simply languish, unheard. There is enormous need for reform within the Dáil and the Senate, and I don't see this happening without a serious injection of new blood.

I am thoroughly disgruntled with political fiefdoms, the attitude that 'this is a Cowan seat' or 'this is an Andrews seat'. I hate that – it reminds me of the rotten boroughs in nineteenth-century England before the reform of the House of Commons. The idea that the sister, widow, son or brother of the former TD is a virtual shoo-in for nomination is something that should be left in the past, and means that those of us who live in that constituency are essentially being disenfranchised.

Another thing that I am tired of is the fact that there are people within Dáil Éireann who have demonstrated a serious lack of integrity by their own actions, and yet they still hold high office in our country. I do not understand this and I think it is a pity.

Politics needs to attract people who wish to confront national issues and tread the national stage, even if they aren't necessarily keen on coming up through the system of local councillors (who certainly have a job to do, but I would argue are too numerous, and that anyway national politics should be a very different beast). Too much of Irish politics is parish pump politics. I heard it said by the late Justin Keating when he was in the cabinet as Minister for Industry and Commerce, that, as a TD, if you are faced with a choice between being in Dáil Éireann to debate a bill of national significance, or going to the funeral of a local businessman or GAA player, you go to the funeral because that's where the votes are.

To me, this is ridiculous. No wonder there is such a lack of political excitement among the young in this country. And the quality of debate within the Dáil chamber is often very poor, something that astounds me in a country where nearly every person I meet in the daily course of my life uses English so expressively. Why, therefore, are our politicians unable to put forward a robust, articulate argument? I am articulate and very used to debate and public speaking, whether in front of audiences, on radio or TV. It has happened, quite organically it seems to me, that I have become an early port of call for media outlets looking to make sense of certain HSE decisions, or for someone who can put forward the reasons why some of these decisions are so wrong. As an Independent I would not be subject to the government whip system, by which the speaker is told who can and cannot respond to questions, and I run no risk of putting other party members' noses out of joint. This can happen all too easily when someone is parachuted in because they have an existing public profile, only for them to find that there are a couple of bitter colleagues lurking in the background who felt the job was theirs and are consequently furious.

My plan is to stand, and if elected, go in just for one term. In doing so, I wish to achieve two things by fighting for what I believe in (unshakeable integrity as a given): dignity for all our citizens and independence of mind. My politics are liberal right. What that means in effect is that I believe in people and their ability to influence their own circumstances. I want to show by example that individuals can challenge the sprawling democracy and effect change. That we are not entirely subject to the whim and will of the state.

I wish to take the lessons learned from creating the Jack and Jill Foundation and write them large. These lessons show that it is possible to change direction at any stage in one's life; to take on new challenges and succeed at them. It is possible to take a situation that seems hopeless and improve it out of all recognition. It is possible to find money privately that has not been made available by government to fund these projects. It is possible to scale up a project that is proven to work on a small level and make it nationally significant. It is possible to affect government policy, to some extent at least, by demonstrating best practice. Passion, enthusiasm and a determination never to hear no, can jump a lot of hurdles.

Additionally, I hope to inspire young people within all constituencies to believe they can outwit the party system and take up the fight. I'm not saying I can change the world, but I can certainly shake the tiger by the tail. Shane Ross, Mattie McGrath and Finian McGrath have shown that you can achieve as an Independent. People trust their integrity and effectiveness. I would love to think that the system will never be the same again, that if I succeed, I will show that things can change. I know one Independent can't change everything, but I want to get in there and shake things up.

Even on what might sound like a foolish level, I would like to get the catering changed in Leinster House. It is a wonderful forum to bring important members of the business, legal, educational, sport and entertainment communities into, and give them lunch in the beautiful dining room. That room should be full every day with the people who pull the levers in this country. But the food just doesn't measure up to its surroundings. It is a great shame that the world never steps into Leinster House unless there for constituency visits. It should be more open and more accessible. There should be provision made for less formal public engagement with the place. I wish the enterprise and commercial spirit shown by some of the semi-state bodies such as Bord Bia and Enterprise Ireland could be transferred to the civil service. We are a young country, with deep-rooted traditions and yet, at the opening of the twenty-first century, our system of managing the country seems very old-fashioned and very bloated.

One of my most immediate concerns if I succeed in being elected will be reform of the charity sector. After all, who better to reform something than an insider? Charity now has moved on to become an industry in its own right, yet the sector has very little credibility, something we saw all too clearly recently during the scandal around top-up payments for executive members at the Central Remedial Clinic (CRC). I am enraged by what happened there, but not at all surprised. Jack and Jill is a young charity and has always been vociferous about the reform of the charity sector and the need for a regulator. Mary-Ann has been leading the same charge in the Senate, having met with both the chairman of the Scottish Charity Regulator and the UK Charity Commission to understand best practice.

Sadly, what happened with the CRC, for example, is something that she and I foresaw, because there is no control over where the vast sums of charity money go. If the sector had been properly regulated from the start it would have been impossible for senior management to access any of the charitable funds. It simply couldn't have happened. But in the absence of regulation, with €4 billion of government money sloshing about in the sector every year, I am sure there are many other equally appalling stories that we haven't yet heard about. I have never quite got over my shock on first attending a major charitable conference in Croke Park, to see up on the screen the figure of 67 per cent as the average grant by the state to charities, knowing that Jack and Jill gets only 18 per cent; there are clearly charities who are getting nearly 100 per cent.

On a brighter note, this spring saw legislation enacted that now allows for a charity regulator, together with a board and full office, to properly police the sector, enacted by Alan Shatter as Minister for Justice, with important input from Mary-Ann in her role as senator. Mr Shatter's term as Minister for Justice may have ended disappointingly, but I hope history will be kind to him. The vitriolic hatred expressed when he resigned was unjustified. When it comes to criticism of the gift of €70,000 that he gave to Jack and Jill, as I see it he had three options: take the money, leave it in the maw of the state, or give it to charity. In my opinion he made the right decision.

The pillars of our society are crumbling. The banks are discredited, so are the religious, the lawyers, and now charity. Until recently, charity work was perceived as something fine and upstanding, but that too has now got tired. Donations to the Jack and Jill Foundation didn't suffer during the top-up scandal, I think because we are like a very sad, very mini kind of GAA. Our babies are in many parishes in the country; we are local, grassroots, and so is our support. But it is very clear to me that proper full regulation of the sector is long overdue.

Something else that motivates me at a profound level, mainly inspired by deep, deep irritation, is the on-going mess around the much-needed National Children's Hospital. Now twenty years in the planning, with €50 million spent, and still not one single brick laid, this is appalling, ridiculous and shaming. It is also costing lives and contributing to great distress among sick children and their families.

I feel so strongly about this that I am not prepared to wait until the election to tackle it. It was while I was lying in St Vincent's Private, recovering from my cancer operation, that I began to think, 'Here I am in the most outstanding hospital, built by private enterprise, delivered on time, on budget and with no fuss.' So I have begun to put together a syndicate and a plan for a state-of-the-art hospital, located on the greenfield site where James Connolly Memorial Hospital is already situated, in Blanchardstown. It is easily accessible off the M50, with plenty of space not only for the Children's Hospital as currently conceived, but also for later expansion and the siting of the new National Maternity Hospital, which is also badly needed and which is currently being suggested for the car park of St Vincent's.

Why none of the officials involved in managing the plans for these hospitals understand the importance of car parking, I do not understand. The site currently planned for the Children's Hospital is the car park of St James's Hospital – why must they make a club sandwich of all our hospitals? Do they not think it important that people have somewhere to park? Or indeed that the many people travelling from outside Dublin – and 73 per cent of our Jack and Jill families live outside Dublin – would welcome not having to navigate the medieval streets of Dublin, but rather take an easy exit off the M50; always remembering that 92 per cent of sick children travel to hospital by car.

If I can put this together at the site in Blanchardstown, we will have an operational hospital, delivered and ready to go in 2018. At the best assessment, the government won't be ready until 2020, and if they do have a hospital by then there won't be space to park your car. Blanchardstown has space, in sylvan surrounds, for the Children's Hospital, the Maternity Hospital and a research building all on one modern campus. We plan also to re-establish James Connolly Memorial Hospital as a fully operational front-rank tertiary adult hospital. There is no point setting up a hospital that works for today, without looking at what the needs will be in twenty, thirty or forty years time. This cannot be the kind of short-term approach that we have taken too often in this country. We need to think big and think long-term, and do it right, from the start.

The independent Dolphin Report commissioned by the government to examine different site possibilities, found James Connolly Memorial Hospital to have one negative – the lack of public transport, e.g. no LUAS line (Dublin's light rail system) – whereas the St James's site had more negatives. It is clearly the most suitable site, but somehow it wasn't chosen, losing out to St James's for reasons that we are not privy to. The Dolphin Report lacked any scoring formula or weighting system, allowing politicians a free run at the eventual choice.

I have a huge belief in the concept that Lord Beveridge used to create the welfare state, but I think that now we need to move away from feeling, 'Oh, the state will take care of everything,' because the state won't and our children are too precious to allow our politicians and a dysfunctional HSE to be in charge of. This is the moment for private enterprise to step up and contribute on a grand scale, in the way that wealthy individuals do in countries like the United States, where there is an established tradition of philanthropy, and did in Ireland in the nineteenth century.

For those private investors who do get involved, the return is mainly honour and glory. My ideal would be to create a social bond – something that is very common in America, for example – which carries slightly higher interest rates than the banks offer, redeemable in five years, with all income exempt from taxation. The cheapest bond would cost, say €100, so that every family in the country who wanted to, could be part of the National Children's Hospital, at a tiny cost. Probably those who purchase €100 or €200 worth of bonds will never redeem them, they are getting involved for reasons of conscience rather than financial reasons, but for those who invest several million the financial incentives are attractive. Even so, philanthropy will probably be their driving motivation. For those who donate such large sums, we would have no problem in calling a wing after them, or their mother or father, for example. And I feel it is not unreasonable to ask these people, who have made very large sums of money, to fund a children's hospital.

Built by private enterprise, we would not be beholden to any particular medical or political faction. And once we have the funds for the hospital to be built, I have no doubt the government will accept our proposal. Of course, there is no guarantee of that, but it would be mighty strange if they didn't when we would have saved them so much money. They will not have to find in excess of €400 million to add to the €200 million already ear-marked from the sale of the National Lottery for the creation of a Children's Hospital (the up-to-date cost of the HSE site at St James's is €690 million – almost certainly unaffordable).

I am happy to put together a syndicate to build it and hand the keys to the HSE, but I will not allow them to be involved in the design of the hospital or project management.

Right now, what I'm looking for is the Gabriel to lead the charge among the angels: the one person who will put money into the project, and will pick up the phone to encourage others to join them. I have never felt more strongly about anything than I do about this. Ireland needs a decent children's hospital – Crumlin will be closed in ten years and Temple Street is inadequate. All of my dealings with the government so far, in the seventeen years since I set up the Jack and Jill Foundation, as well as my previous career in horse racing, inclines me to believe that they will be unable to do this most important job as well as a private venture could. And I cannot rest until I have tried to see what I can do to make this happen.

When I first moved to Ireland in 1959, to go to Trinity College, I presumed my future lay in England. In as much as I had a plan at all, it was probably to complete my education and go back to London. Instead, the mercurial Wing Commander Tim Vigors set me on a new path that took me to the heart of the Irish bloodstock industry, on which I feel I left a considerable and positive impression, to the long-term benefit of that industry; and then, through the tragic accident of Jack's birth and death, into a sector I could never have imagined having anything to do with – charity. Only the fact that I discovered, at first hand, just how little the government was prepared to care for the most vulnerable children born within the state, has led to me becoming deeply immersed in this sad world.

Through the Jack and Jill Foundation we have made that world a little less sad, a little less neglected and a little less ignored, bringing 'the gift of time' to deeply traumatised families. At an age when many are considering retirement and winding down, I would now like to bring what we have learned through Jack and Jill into national politics. Ireland has always been a good friend to me, a wonderful place to live, and I would like to return the favour as best I can.

Appendix

A Jack and Jill Family Story

John and Catherine O'Leary are parents of Jack, aged five, and Tom, aged three, who has trisomy 7p, a rare chromosomal disorder.

John is area sales manager for Permanent TSB, and was goalkeeper for the Dublin football team for eighteen years. He won two All-Ireland medals, in 1983 and again, as captain, in 1995. Catherine gave up work after Tom was born because he needed constant care. John told their story to Emily Hourican.

Tom was born in October 2010, three weeks early. That didn't seem like a problem as Jack was born four weeks early and was perfectly healthy. Tom was born by emergency section because the birth wasn't progressing as it should, after which medical staff took him away and checked him out. They said he was a bit floppy and took him to an incubator. At that point we didn't think anything was particularly wrong, but, in retrospect, from that moment on it was as if we had stepped onto an out-of-control train, where the news we got just seemed to get worse and worse.

Tom was checked for Down's syndrome and we were told that he didn't have that, but that he had a heart murmur and would need surgery. That wasn't the best news, but we assumed it was a question of getting surgery and fixing the problem, after which Tom would have a perfectly normal life.

Then we were told that he had trisomy 7p, a rare chromosomal disorder where a piece of chromosome 7 breaks off and sticks onto chromosome 15. The condition is so rare that there isn't any real prognosis in terms of what to expect. We brought Tom home at the start of November, but we quickly realised that he wasn't feeding well, sometimes taking as little as 5 or 10 ml, and he clearly wasn't thriving. He got very sick late in November and we took him to Crumlin Hospital, where he stayed for almost a month and, as we later heard, nearly died. He had some kind of infection and his white-blood-cell count went through the roof. At Crumlin they told us that Tom was aspirating some of each feed, that it was getting into his lungs, and that was why he kept getting severe chest infections.

Eventually, Tom came home on Christmas Eve, but soon it was clear that he wasn't putting on weight. He had to get to 5 kg before they would consider performing heart surgery. So three months later he was back in Crumlin, on a nasal and IV drip to feed him, so as to bring his weight up. We tried to be with him every hour that he was in there, which puts so much strain on family life. We used to sit there at night, watching cars going by on the road outside, thinking we used to be like that – people who just drove past Crumlin Hospital without thinking about what goes on in here. It is like a parallel universe in there. The nurses and frontline staff are wonderful, but have the HSE managers ever spent a day on a ward, seeing what actually happens? Probably not, or they wouldn't be so harsh in their treatment of families who need help.

It was then that the Jack and Jill Foundation came into our lives. We had heard of them, although we didn't know what they did, but someone suggested that Tom might be the kind of baby they could help, and so Sinéad Moran, the liaison nurse, contacted us and that journey took off.

Tom had his heart operation on 15 March and that went fine. In mid-April he had another operation to insert a PEG into his stomach through which he is still fed a specialised high-calorie food. In the beginning it took about two hours to feed him and he needed to be fed five times a day. So almost as one feed finished, the next was due.

Tom needed twenty-four-hour care. He has sleep apnoea and requires oxygen, particularly at night. He still can't walk or talk and is developmentally behind. Caring for him is very intense and so he can't be left with the usual people who would normally mind children, such as grandparents, neighbours and friends. They want to help, but can't. That means that popping out to the shops for half an hour becomes a major operation, or if the weather is bad and only one of us is at home, we can't go, because the chance of Tom getting a chest infection is not worth taking. He doesn't fight infection well, so he gets sick easily and minor infections become very serious.

Jack and Jill give us nursing hours, and therefore freedom and rest. Their nurses will mind Tom while we get a night's sleep or have a day out. And these nurses are amazing: they dedicate themselves to the kids and love their jobs. We got married last May, and that couldn't have happened without one of their nurses to mind Tom. In the months before Jack and Jill came into our lives our eldest son, Jack, was being passed around from pillar to post, to grandparents, friends, anyone who would take him for a couple of hours or a night while we were in Crumlin with Tom. Even when we were at home with him, playing, we always had one eye on Tom's beepers and monitors, and were liable to be interrupted at any moment by him vomiting or turning blue. Jack was getting upset because he wasn't able to do things with us or have his needs tended to, and we felt constantly guilty because of what he was missing out on. Now, we are able to take him to the zoo, out to McDonald's, normal kid's stuff. And he has a role to play in minding Tom – Jack's job is to get the sick-tray when Tom vomits, as he so often does.

Jack and Jill have given us confidence, as parents, with Tom. Sinéad is always on the end of the phone to talk to, to ask questions of and be reassured by. If Tom is turning blue, losing weight, getting sick, we can ring her and she will talk us through everything. Does he need oxygen? Does he need suction? We can now do these things ourselves. Without Jack and Jill to turn to, Tom would definitely spend far more time in Crumlin. When Jonathan says he saves the HSE money through the work that Jack and Jill does, he is absolutely right. With Sinéad there to talk to, often every day or second day, and check our own assessment with, we have learned to trust our own judgement around what Tom needs and, as a result, he spends far less time in hospital.

The other side of Jack and Jill is the social side, the chance to meet other parents with children like Tom. That has helped hugely with the sense of isolation we suffered at first. We found other people to talk to, who know what you're going through. For example, in some ways, having a child with disabilities is like having a baby forever. There is no question of that child sleeping through the night: it's never going to happen. To hear other parents talking about their four-month-old, say, and how he sleeps eight hours, just brings it home that you will never have that.

There is no long-term prognosis for Tom. His condition is unique – on a UK database of chromosomal mismatches and swap-overs of around 8,000 people, Tom is the only one with his specific mismatch. That means there is no road map, no way of anticipating what might happen. You just have to roll with it. From our point of view that is a good thing, because it means we are not waiting for some dreadful day when he's, say, six and going to die, for example. We just have to take everything day by day.

Tom can now get around by himself, by doing a bum shuffle. This has been a massive landmark for us. We have no idea how much more he will be capable of, but already the interaction between him and Jack has progressed to the kind of normal rough and tumble between brothers, although obviously we have to be very careful always. We always believe that we are very lucky with Tom. There are so many children we know through Jack and Jill who are far worse off.

Next October Tom turns four and we will lose the support

of the Jack and Jill Foundation. We are already dreading that day, and not just because of the minding of him, but the support, the help, the back-up that comes with that. We will then be at the mercy of the HSE, even though Jack and Jill have already begun the process of trying to get us nursing hours from it. Sadly, the HSE behave as if they simply don't care, that somehow it is our fault that we have a child like Tom and we shouldn't be bothering them for help. Why they behave like this towards the people who are in desperate need of help and kindness is impossible to figure out. Fortunately, we both have very positive dispositions, because you could get really angry, really down about it, and you need your energy for your sick child, not for fighting institutions.

We have given back what we can. We have fund-raised, and so have all our friends and family, and we have been into the Dáil with Jonathan to make the case to the politicians there. We have been on TV and radio to publicise the amazing work Jack and Jill do.

Jonathan probably doesn't even realise half of his value to us. He does this because that's what he does – it comes naturally to him. But when you think of the number of families he has helped, and how much he has helped them, it is amazing. He is humble and doesn't look for praise, but where would we be without Jack and Jill? Nowhere good.

Jonathan calls Tom and all the Jack and Jill children 'his' children, and they are. He's like a father to all of them. He loves them, every single one of them, and he fights constantly, in the background, for them.

There are no words to describe the help Jack and Jill has given us. We never thought we would have a child with special needs – no one ever does, you never think it will be you – but when it happened, Jack and Jill saved our family.

To find out more about
the Jack & Jill Children's
Foundation please go to
www.jackandjill.ie

MERCIER PRESS
IRISH PUBLISHER - IRISH STORY

We hope you enjoyed this book.

Since 1944, Mercier Press has published books that have been critically important to Irish life and culture.

Our website is the best place to find out more information about Mercier, our books, authors, news and the best deals on a wide variety of books. Mercier tracks the best prices for our books online and we seek to offer the best value to our customers, offering free delivery within Ireland.

A large selection of Mercier's new releases and backlist are also available as ebooks. We have an ebook for everyone, with titles available for the Amazon Kindle, Sony Reader, Kobo Reader, Apple products and many more. Visit our website to find and buy our ebooks.

Sign up on our website or complete and return the form below to receive updates and special offers.

www.mercierpress.ie
www.facebook.com/mercier.press
www.twitter.com/irishpublisher

Name: _____

Email: _____

Address: _____

Mobile No.: _____

Mercier Press, Unit 3b, Oak House, Bessboro Rd, Blackrock, Cork, Ireland